SAY IT IN

CROATIAN

Pocket Phrase Book and Dictionary

BY
RUŽICA KAPETANOVIĆ

Associated Book Publishers, Inc.

P. O. Box 5657

Scottsdale, AZ 85261-5657

ISBN: 0-910164-26-6

Printed in the United States of America

TABLE OF CONTENTS

INTRODUCTION

With its natural beauty and magic charm Croatia has been a favorite travel destination for decades. Over the centuries Croatia has been visited by royalty, aristocracy and nobility from all five continents. Some came publicly, some came secretly, some came invited and many came uninvited. The country has been occupied by Tatars, Avars, Venetians, Austrians, Hungarians, Turks and Serbs. All had a desire to own Croatia and wanted to conquer her rich and beautiful land. Popular with aristocracy and simple folks alike, anyone who has visited Croatia, even briefly, need not be convinced to come again.

Whether you plan to go to Croatia as a tourist, a diplomat or to conduct business, this phrase book will be very helpful to you. It contains phrases that you will use every day during your travels throughout Croatian-speaking areas. Learning some Croatian before and during your trip will make it more enjoyable and will help you to get closer to the people you meet and to make lasting friendships.

Only those words and phrases that are essential to the traveller have been included in this book. In choosing the vocabulary and expressions, we have taken into account the ease with which the English-language speaker could pronounce and remember the terms in question. For that reason, we have in certain instances substituted anglicized or international words for some Croatian words. Although purists may feel that this is not absolutely 'correct' literary Croatian, this provides the greatest ease in communicating for the average speaker of English.

The phrases are divided into several sections, each dealing with a different situation that might be encountered while travelling. Some phrases are included in several sections because they are crucial to making oneself understood in various situations. A small dictionary is provided at the end of the book to help the user easily find Croatian words and phrases he might encounter and to provide access to additional vocabulary.

Say It In Croatian includes a guide to Croatian pronunciation and a very brief review of Croatian grammar, covering the most essential points. You will find it a great help to read these sections prior to using the phrase book, although studying the material in depth is not crucial.

In many cases the phrases provide alternative words that may be used in the same context, or the phrases are provided both as a negative and a positive expression. In these instances the alternative words or phrases are separated by a slash as in the following example:

> *This is/is not my luggage.*
> **Ovo je/nije moja prtljaga.**

Similarly, there is often a different ending for expressions uttered by a woman from those uttered by a man. In such cases again the difference is indicated by a slash separating the feminine form of the word from the masculine or separating the feminine ending from the masculine. Throughout the book the masculine form is provided first, then the feminine as in the following examples:

I am tired.
Ja sam umoran/umorna.

I am a Croatian.
Jam sam Hrvat/ica.

If you are not understood the first time, try repeating the phrase. Don't be overly concerned about being absolutely correct in pronunciation. Native speakers of any language expect a foreigner to pronounce their language slightly differently. Just do your best. The effort that you put out in trying to speak Croatian will be greatly appreciated and the people you are trying to communicate with will try their best to be courteous and helpful to you.

In certain instances you might not have the time or you might become too tongue-tied to read the proper phrase from the book. In such instances it would be fine to point to the English phrase in the book. The Croatian speaker will understand what you are trying to communicate by reading its Croatian equivalent.

Your comments, criticisms and suggestions would be greatly appreciated in helping us to prepare future editions. Please direct all your correspondence to the author in care of Associated Book Publishers, Inc.

Hvala. Sretan Put!

GUIDE TO PRONUNCIATION

No transcriptions for Croatian pronunciation are provided in this book because Croatian is written phonetically. Once the pronunciation of each letter is learned, every word can be sounded out without difficulty. For that reason, we recommend spending a little time learning to pronounce the letters of the Croatian alphabet. This should not be difficult because the letters are relatively easy to pronounce. Below is the Croatian alphabet with a sample word containing that letter. Also included is a word that provides the closest sound in an English word.

Letter	Sample Word	English Equivalent
A a	Ante	a as in aunt
B b	Buje	b as in boy
C c	Crikvenica	ts as in cats
Č č	Čakovec	ch as in church
Ć ć	ćuk	ty as in future
D d	Daruvar	d as in dog
Dž dž	džezva	j as in judge
Đ đ	Đakovo	dj as in soldier
E e	Engleska	e as in get
F f	Foča	f as in fog
G g	Glina	g as in go
H h	Hrvatska	h as in hat
I i	Imotski	ee as in eagle
J j	Jelisavac	y as in yes

K k	Korčula	k as in keep
L l	Labin	l as in lamp
Lj lj	Ljubica	ly as in brilliant
M m	Mostar	m as in man
N n	Našice	n as in no
Nj nj	Njemačka	ny as in onion
O o	Osijek	o as in open
P p	Pag	p as in pop
R r	Rijeka	trilled 'r' *
S s	Sisak	s as in sit
Š š	Šibenik	sh as in shoe
T t	Trogir	t as in top
U u	Una	oo as in zoom
V v	Vukovar	v as in van
Z z	Zagreb	z as in zebra
Ž ž	Županja	zh as in pleasure

*The letter 'r' is the only sound which can function as either a consonant or a vowel in Croatian. It is a trilled sound which means that the tongue vibrates against the upper gum ridge. This allows it to be produced between consonants in words like the following:

Krk   vrt   prst   trg

A similar sound is produced after the sound *th* by Scottish speakers of English in such words as *three* or *through*.

Long and Short Vowels:

Croatian vowels may be long or short, depending on the words in which they occur. English also has long and short vowels, but their occurence is determined by the consonant which follows the vowel, thus the pronunciation of a long or short vowel usually does not affect the meaning of the word. For example, compare the pronunciation of the vowels in the English words *hat* and *had*. The sound of the '**a**' in the word *had* is considerably longer than the sound of the '**a**' in the word *hat*. English follows a pattern whereby all vowels are short when followed by the sound '**t**' and long when followed by the sound '**d**'. Although one would sound a little bit strange, pronouncing the word *hat* with a long vowel or the word *had* with a short vowel, it does not result in a difference in meaning.

In Croatian differences in long and short vowels can produce a difference in meaning. Thus the word *luk* pronounced with a short vowel means 'onion' while the word *luk* pronounced with a long vowel means 'arch'.

Accents

In addition to long and short vowels, differences in accents may result in different meanings in Croatian. In English, where the stress falls may distinguish the meaning of certain words. For example, the word *inVAlid* means not valid, but the word *INvalid* means someone with a disability. Similarly, in Croatian accenting one or another syllable may result in a different meaning. For example, the expression *pa da (pa DA)* means 'yes, of course' while the word *pada (PAda)* means 'it falls'.

Although the length of the vowels and the accent on the vowels is more significant in Croatian than it is in English, written Croatian does not mark the stress or the shortness of the vowel. For that reason, we have chosen not to indicate accent marks in the Croatian text. We feel that adding accent marks would serve to confuse the casual speaker of Croatian more than it would serve to clarify how to pronounce Croatian words and phrases. Differentiating words by accent is so alien to English that speakers of

English are often inhibited in their attempts to produce them. As you listen to Croatian try to imitate the accents. A little practice goes a long way. The phrases and words in this book are all very basic. You will be understood even if you miss an accent here and there.

GREETINGS AND SALUTATIONS

The first expressions that you will want to learn in Croatian will undoubtedly be for greeting people. The following are short greetings that you will find simple to learn and to use when you meet people in Croatia, in your own country, or while travelling, perhaps on a plane or on a ship.

Good Morning.
Dobro Jutro.

Good Evening.
Dobar Večer.

Good Afternoon.
Dobar Dan.

Good Night.
Laku noć.

Good Day.
Dobar Dan.

Good luck!
Sretno!

How are you?
Kako ste?

Fine, thank you and you?
Dobro, hvala, a Vi?

How is Mr. ...?
Kako je Gospodin ...?

How is Mrs. ...?
Kako je Gospođa ...?

May I present Mr. ...
Dopustite da Vam predstavim Gospodina ...

This is my husband.
Ovo je moj suprug.

This is my wife.
Ovo je moja supruga.

This is my friend. (male)
Ovo je moj prijatelj.

This is my friend. (female)
Ovo je moja prijateljica.

This is my mother, and my father.
Ovo je moja majka, i moj otac.

Introducing...   *This is my brother, and my sister.*
Ovo je moj brat, i moja sestra.

Those are my parents.   *Is this your daughter/son?*
To su moji roditelji.   **Je li ovo Vaša kći/Vaš sin?**

Pleased to meet you.
Drago mi je.

I hope that we will meet again.
Nadam se da ćemo se opet vidjeti.

See you tomorrow.
Vidimo se sutra.

I beg your pardon?
Molim?

Yes   No
Da   Ne

Excuse me./Pardon me.
Oprostite.

OK/Fine/Alright.
Dobro.

I'm very sorry.
Žao mi je.

Please.
Molim.

Thank you.
Hvala.

You're welcome.
Molim.

With pleasure.
Rado.

Don't mention it.
Nema na čemu.

See you later.
Vidimo se.

Good bye.
Do viđenja.
Zbogom.

Have a good trip!
Sretan put!

Good luck./All the best.
Sve najbolje.

GENERAL EXPRESSIONS

This section contains those expressions which are very useful and will be used again and again. Especially important are those expressions which express desire or volition. By substituting a word or a phrase, they are used in many varied situations. For that reason, it would be a good idea to become thoroughly familiar at least with these expressions, along with greetings and salutations.

Welcome.
Dobro došli.

Welcome to Croatia.
Dobro došli u Hrvatsku.

What is your name?
Kako se (Vi) zovete?

My name is....
Ja se zovem...

What is his (her) name?
Kako se on(a) zove?

What is your last name?
Kako se prezivate?

My last name is...
Ja se prezivam...

Where do you live?
Gdje živite?

I reside here.
Stanujem ovdje.

I live in America.
Živim u Americi.

I	You (familiar & sing.)		You (formal & plural)	
Ja	**Ti**		**Vi**	

We	He	She	They (masc)	They (fem.)
Mi	**On**	**Ona**	**Oni**	**One**

Who?	My	Your (sing.)	Your (pl.)	His
Tko?	**Moj**	**Tvoj**	**Vaš**	**Njegov**

Her	Our	Their	Whose?
Njezin	**Naš**	**Njihov**	**Čiji?**

Do you know him [her]?
Poznate li njega [nju]?

Yes, I know him [her].
Da, poznam ga [nju].

No, I don't know him [her].
Ne, ne poznam ga [nju].

I [don't] know you.
Ja Vas [ne] poznam.

At which hotel are you staying?
U kojem ste hotelu?

Do you know where he lives?
Znate li gdje on stanuje?

I don't know.
Neznam.

Do you speak English?
Govorite li engleski?

ŠTO IMA NOVOGA?

What's new?
Što ima novoga?

I don't speak Croatian.
Ja ne govorim hrvatski.

Please say it in English.
Molim Vas recite na engleskom.

Does anyone here speak English?
Ima li nekoga ovdje tko govori engleski?

Do you understand?	*Yes, I understand.*
Razumijete li?	**Da, razumijem.**

No, I don't understand.	*I understand a little.*
Ne, ne razumijem.	**Razumijem malo.**

I don't understand everything.
Ne razumijem sve.

Please speak more slowly.
Molim Vas, govorite polakše.

Please repeat.	*What did you say?*
Molim Vas, ponovite.	**Što ste rekli?**

How do you say that in Croatian?
Kako se to kaže na hrvatskom?

Bring me...	*Give me....*
Donesite mi....	**Dajte mi....**

Send me...	*Tell me....*
Pošaljite mi....	**Recite mi...**

Show me...	*I need....*
Pokažite mi....	**Trebam....**

I would like...	*I want...*
Želim...	**Ja hoću...**

I don't want...	*I can...*
Ja neću....	**Ja mogu...**

I can do that.
Ja to mogu.

I cannot do that.
Ja to ne mogu.

Have you....?
Imate li...?

Are you...?
Jeste li...?

Where is...?
Gdje je...?

Where are...?
Gdje su...?

Where are you going?
Kamo idete?

Where is he [she] going?
Kamo ide on[a]?

Where are we going?
Kamo idemo?

Where is my luggage?
Gdje je moja prtljaga?

Where are the toilets?
Gdje su zahodi?

Ladies' Room.
Ženski zahod.

Men's Room.
Muški zahod.

What does that mean?
Što to znaći?

What do you mean?
Kako mislite?

You are right.
Vi ste u pravu.

He [she] is right.
On [ona] je u pravu.

You are wrong.
Vi niste u pravu.

He is wrong.
On nije u pravu.

Of course.
Sigurno.

Without a doubt.
Bez sumnje.

Wait!
Čekajte!

How long must I wait?
Koliko dugo moram čekati?

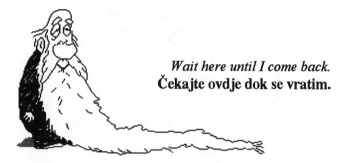

Wait here until I come back.
Čekajte ovdje dok se vratim.

Have you been waiting long?
Čekate li dugo?

Come here.
Dođite ovamo.

I will wait here.
Ja ću čekati ovdje.

I don't want to wait.
Ne želim čekati.

I will not wait.
Neću čekati.

I will wait at the hotel.
Čekat ću u hotelu.

Don't wait for me.
Nemojte me čekati.

Is it near here?
Je li blizu?

Come in!
Uđite!

Is it far from here?
Je li daleko odavde?

It's possible.
To je moguće.

It is not far.
Nije daleko.

It's impossible.
To je nemoguće.

Who is he [she]?
Tko je on[a]?

Who are they?
Tko su oni/one?

Who is that boy /girl?
Tko je taj dečko/ta djevojka?

Who is that man/woman?
Tko je taj čovjek/ta žena?

That is my brother/sister.
To je moj brat/moja sestra.

That is my wife/husband.
To je moja supruga/moj suprug.

*That is my friend. (*male)*
To je moj prijatelj.

*That is my friend. (*female)*
To je moja prijateljica.

Those are my friends.
To su moji prijatelji.

I would like to meet him/her.
Želim ga/ju upoznati.

She's a pretty woman.
Ona je lijepa žena.

She's a pretty girl.
Ona je lijepa djevojka.

He's a handsome man.
On je zgodan čovjek.

He's a handsome young man.
On je zgodan momak.

CUSTOMS AND BORDERS

No matter how you travel to Croatia, you will have to go through passport and customs formalities. In this section you will find the expressions that you will need to get you through as quickly as possible so that you may be off to your hotel or other destination in the shortest possible time.

Your passport, please.
Putovnicu molim.

Here is my passport.
Izvolite moju putovnicu.

How long will you be staying in Croatia?
Koliko ćete dugo boraviti u Hrvatskoj?

I will stay in Croatia only a few days.
Bit ću u Hrvatskoj samo nekoliko dana.

...three weeks.
...tri tjedna.

...two months.
...dva mjeseca.

Why have you come to Croatia?
Zašto ste došli u Hrvatsku?

I am just passing through.
Samo prolazim.

I am a tourist.
Ja sam turist.

I have come on holiday.
Došao/došla sam na odmor.

I have come on business.
Došao/došla sam poslovno.

Here is my business card.
Izvolite moju posjetnicu.

I am an American/Canadian/British citizen.
Ja sam američki/kanadski/britanski državljanin.

Have you anything to declare?
Imate li što za prijaviti?

I have nothing to declare.
Nemam ništa za prijaviti.

Are these your bags?
Je li ovo Vaša prtljaga?

Yes, and here are the keys.
Da, evo su i ključevi.

Open this box.
Otvorite ovu kutiju.

Open/close your bags.
Otvorite/zatvorite prtljagu.

Have you any cigarettes or tobacco?
Imate li cigareta ili duhana?

I have only cigarettes.
Imam samo cigareta.

This is for my personal use.
Ovo je za moju vlastitu uporabu.

You must pay duty.
Morate platiti carinu.

How much must I pay?
Koliko moram platiti?

May I go now?
Mogu li ići sada?

Is that all?
Je li to sve?

You may go now.
Sada možete ići.

Porter, please carry this luggage.
Nosaču, molim Vas, uzmite ovu prtljagu.

Is this your suitcase?
Je li ovo Vaš kovčeg?

No, that is not mine.
Ne, to nije moj.

COMMUNICATIONS

Communications are handled in Croatia through the Croatian Post and Telecommunications–HPT (Hrvatska pošta i telekomunikacije.) Calling from public telephone booths has been simplified by the use of electronic telephone cards which can be purchased at the post office. The telephone card has a certain value and as calls are made the value remaining on the card is decreased. This is convenient for making out of city or long distance calls from a pay phone because no coins or tokens are required to make the call.

USING THE TELEPHONE

Is there a telephone here?
Ima li telefon ovdje?

May I use the telephone?
Mogu li koristiti telefon?

Where is there a telephone booth?
Gdje ima govornica?

I would like to make a call to Canada.
Želim zvati Kanadu.

...a Croatian restaurant.
...hrvatski restoran.

...the American embassy.
...američku ambasadu.

...Hotel Park..
...Hotel Park.

Where can I buy telephone cards?
Gdje mogu kupiti telefonske kartice?

At the post office.
U pošti.

What is the telephone number you wish to call?
Koji je broj telefona koji želite zvati?

Where is the telephone book?
Gdje je telefonski imenik?

I want to call home.
Želim zvati doma.

What time is it in California?
Koliko je sati u Kaliforniji?

I would like to call the United States collect.
Želim zvati Ameriku na njihov račun.

I want number....   *Can I dial this number?*
Želim zvati broj....   **Mogu li ja nazvati ovaj broj?**

How much is a telephone call to...?
Koliko je naziv u...?

I am ringing...
Zovem...

Please connect me with the Palace Hotel.
Molim Vas spojite me sa Palace Hotelom.

I have gotten the wrong number.
Dobio/dobila sam krivi broj.

Please do not hang up.
Molim Vas nemojte spustiti slušalicu.

I was cut off. Can you reconnect me?
Prekinulo me. Možete li me ponovo spojiti?

There is no answer.
Nema odgovora.

Please dial again.
Molim Vas, nazovite ponovo.

The line is busy.
Linija je zauzeta.

Thank you. I'll try calling later.
Hvala. Pokušat ću zvati kasnije.

Hello, I want 555-234 please.
Halo, molim Vas želim broj 555-234.

Hello, who is speaking?
Halo, tko govori?

Do you speak English?
Govorite li engleski?

I don't speak Croatian.
Ja ne govorim hrvatski.

Please speak English.
Molim Vas, govorite engleski.

May I speak to...?
Mogu li razgovarati sa...?

He/she is not in.
On/ona nije ovdje.

When will he/she be back?
Kada će se vratiti?

Please leave him/her a message.
Molim Vas ostavite mu/joj poruku.

Tell him/her that ... telephoned.
Recite mu/joj da je zvao/zvala...

Please ask him /her to call me.
Molim Vas recite mu/joj neka me zove.

What is your number?
Koji je Vaš broj?

My number is...
Moj je broj...

Please speak more slowly.
Molim Vas govorite polakše.

Are there any messages for me?
Ima li kakve poruke za mene?

Yes, Mr. Bašić called.
Da, zvao je G. Bašić.

Here is his number.
Evo njegov broj.

This telephone is out of order.
Ovaj telefon ne radi.

POSTAL SERVICES

Can I mail a letter from the hotel?
Mogu li poslati pismo iz hotela?

Where is the [nearest] post office?
Gdje je [najbliža] pošta?

What time does it open?
U koliko sati otvori?

When does it close?
Kada zatvori?

It closes at five.
Zatvori u pet.

Where can I buy some stamps?
Gdje mogu kupiti poštanske marke?

Please go and ask at that counter.
Molim Vas pitajte na onom šalteru.

I would like to send a letter/post cards.
Želim poslati pismo/razglednice.

Please give me an airmail stamp.
Molim Vas dajte mi marku za zračnu poštu.

Where can I drop these letters?
Gdje mogu baciti ova pisma?

How much is a stamp for this letter?
Koliko je marka za ovo pismo?

I would like to send this letter by registered mail.
Želim poslati ovo pismo registrirano.

I would like ten post cards.
Želim deset razglednica.

Can I insure this parcel?
Mogu li osigurati ovaj paket?

What does the package contain?
Što ima u paketu?

Books and printed matter.
Knjige i tiskane stvari.

Do I need to fill out a customs declaration form?
Trebam li ispuniti carinski obrazac?

Please hold my mail until I call for it.
Molim Vas zadržite moju poštu dok ju ne podignem.

Please forward my mail to Rijeka.
Molim Vas uputite moju poštu za mnom u Rijeku.

TELEGRAMS AND CABLES

I would like to send a telegram to Split.
Želim poslati telegram/brzojav u Split.

This is the address.
Ovo je adresa.

How much do twenty words cost?
Koliko bi stajalo poslati dvadeset riječi?

Please send it immediately.
Molim Vas, pošaljite odmah.

SENDING A FAX

Is there a fax machine in this hotel?
Ima li telekopirni stroj u ovom hotelu?

Can I send a fax from here?
Mogu li poslati telefaks odavde?

Where is there a fax machine I can use?
Gdje ima telekopirni stroj koji mogu upotrijebiti?

How much would it cost to send a page to New York?
Koliko bi stajalo poslati jednu stranicu u New York?

AT THE HOTEL

Whether you stay at a deluxe hotel, a modest hotel or in private accomodations, it is important to be able to express to the staff what you may need or want. The following phrases should provide you with the expressions you will need to make yourself understood in most situations. They may make the difference between settling for whatever you may get or getting what you want.

BOOKING A ROOM

Which is the best hotel?
Koji je najbolji hotel?

I would like to go to Hotel Panorama.
Želim ići u Hotel Panorama.

Please tell me how to get there.
Molim Vas recite mi kako doći tamo.

This is a good hotel.	*I like this hotel.*
Ovo je dobar hotel.	**Meni se sviđa ovaj hotel.**

Rooms to let.	*Do you have a room?*
Sobe za iznajmiti.	**Imate li sobu?**

I have [I don't have] a reservation.
Imam [nemam] rezervaciju.

We have no vacancy.
Nemamo slobodnih soba.

Can you recommend another hotel?
Možete li preporučiti drugi hotel?

Please give me a single room.
Molim Vas dajte mi jednokrevetnu sobu.

...a double room.	*Is there a shower?*
...dvokrevetnu sobu.	**Ima li tuš?**

I want a room ...	*...with/without a bath.*
Želim sobu ...	**...s kupaonom/bez kupaone.**

.... with a view.	*...with air conditioning.*
...s pogledom.	**...s klimatskim uređajem.**

...with a T.V.	*...on the first floor.*
...s televizorom.	**...na prvom katu.**

...that's quiet.	*...which faces the street.*
...koja je tiha.	**...koja gleda prema ulici.**

...close to the elevator.
...blizu lifta.

May I see the room?
Mogu li vidjeti sobu?

This is a large room.
Ovo je velika soba.

This room is too small.
Ova je soba premala.

Do you have a quieter room?
Imate li tišu sobu?

Do you have a room with a view of the sea?
Imate li sobu koja gleda prema moru?

What is the price of this room?   *Are meals included?*
Koliko stoji ova soba?   **Jesu li obroci uračunati?**

Does the price include breakfast?
Je li doručak uračunat?

That's much too expensive.
To je previše skupo.

Where do we register?
Gdje se registrira?

You register over there.
Registrira se tamo.

Please fill out this form/card.
Molim Vas ispunite ovu tiskanicu/kartu.

May I have your passport, please?
Molim Vas, dajte mi Vašu putovnicu.

Is there a restaurant in the hotel?
Ima li restoran u hotelu?

Where is the dining room?
Gdje je blagovaona?

We will stay here.
Ostat ćemo ovdje.

How long will you stay?
Koliko ćete dugo ostati?

I will stay three nights.
Ostat ću tri noći.

We will stay two weeks.
Ostat ćemo dva tjedna.

...overnight
...preko noći.

Where is the key to my room?
Gdje je ključ od moje sobe?

I don't know how long I'll stay.
Neznam koliko ću dugo ostati.

Where is my room?
Gdje je moja soba?

What room number, sir?
Koji broj sobe, gospodine?

Your room is on...
Vaša je soba na...

... the second floor.
...drugom katu.

Our room is on the sixth floor, near the elevator.
Naša je soba na šestom katu, blizu lifta.

I don't like this room.
Ne sviđa mi se ova soba.

I want to change my room.
Želim promijeniti sobu.

This room is...
Ova je soba...

...too small.
...premala.

...too cold.
...previše hladna.

...too warm.
...previše topla.

...too dark.
...previše tamna.

Where is the elevator?
Gdje je lift?

The elevator is on the right/left/over there.
Lift je na desno/na lijevo/tamo.

I am a guest at the Hotel Palace.
Ja sam gost u Palace Hotelu.

Please help me.
Molim Vas pomozite mi.

I am lost.
Ja sam se izgubio/izgubila.

Please help me find my hotel/room.
Molim Vas pomozite mi naći moj hotel/moju sobu.

Where is my luggage?
Gdje je moja prtljaga?

That is my luggage.
To je moja prtljaga.

Please help me with my luggage.
Molim Vas, pomozite mi sa prtljagom.

I have three suitcases.
Imam tri kovčega.

There is a suitcase missing.
Jedan kovčeg nedostaje.

Please send the luggage/suitcase to my room.
Molim Vas pošaljite prtljagu/ kovčeg u moju sobu.

Where's the restaurant?
Gdje je restoran?

Where is the mail box?
Gdje je kutija za poštu?

Where's the post office?
Gdje je pošta?

Where is the bathroom/the toilet?
Gdje je kupaonica/zahod?

Please open the window.
Molim Vas otvorite prozor.

Where can I find...?
Gdje mogu naći...?

Close the window, please.
Zatvorite prozor, molim Vas.

IN THE ROOM

Please call the chambermaid.
Molim Vas, pozovite sobaricu.

I need...
Treba mi...

...a blanket.
...deka.

...a pillow.
...jastuk.

...some hot water.
...vruće vode.

...*some ice.*
...**leda.**

...*a lamp.*
...**lampu.**

...*an ashtray.*
...**pepeonik.**

...*clothes hangers.*
...**vješalice.**

...*stationery.*
...**papir za pisanje pisma.**

...*mineral water.*
...**mineralne vode.**

...*post cards.*
...**razglednice.**

...*stamps.*
...**marke.**

...*an iron.*
...**glačalo.**

...*a hair dryer.*
...**fen za kosu.**

Please bring me a towel and some soap.
Molim Vas donesite mi ručnik i sapuna.

I need a clean towel.
Treba mi čisti ručnik.

There's no plug in the bathtub.
Nema čepa u kadi.

There's no toilet paper in the bathroom.
Nema toaletnog papira u kupaoni.

The toilet doesn't flush.
Školjka ne pušta vodu.

I can't open the window/door.
Ne mogu otvoriti prozor/vrata.

Please open it.
Molim Vas otvorite ga.

Can the heating be turned up/down?
Može li se pojačati/smanjiti grijanje?

Put it on the table, please.
Stavite na stol, molim Vas.

Come in!
Uđite!

This does not work.
Ovo ne radi.

...the door.
...vrata.

...the air-conditioner.
...klimatski uređaj.

...the phone.
...telefon.

...the radio.
...radio.

...the T.V.
...televizor.

...the heat.
...grijanje.

...this light.
...ovo svijetlo.

...the toilet.
...školjka.

...this electric switch.
...ovaj prekidač.

...this electrical outlet.
...ova utičnica.

...the fan.
...ovaj ventilator.

...this faucet.
...ova pipa.

Please repair it.
Molim Vas popravite.

AT THE PORTER'S DESK

I have lost my key.
Izgubio/izgubila sam moj ključ.

...my wallet.
...moju novčarku.

...my wrist watch.
...moj ručni sat.

...my passport.
...moju putovnicu.

...my camera.
...moj slikaći aparat.

...my luggage.
...moju prtljagu.

...my purse.
...moju torbu.

I need a map of the city.
Treba mi plan grada.

My key, please.
Moj ključ, molim Vas.

Is the hotel open all night?
Je li hotel otvoren cijelu noć?

What time does it close?
U koliko sati se zatvori?

Is there any mail for me?
Ima li pošte za mene?

Are there any messages for me?
Ima li kakve poruke za mene?

No one telephoned.
Nitko nije zvao.

DEPARTURE

I will stay another night.
Ostat ću još jednu noć.

We are leaving tomorrow.
Odlazimo sutra.

BRRRINNNNNG

Please wake me at six thirty.
Molim Vas, probudite me u pola sedam.

When is check-out time?
U koliko sati trebamo izići iz sobe?

Take my luggage down.
Odnesite moju prtljagu dolje.

Please prepare my bill.
Molim Vas pripremite račun.

How much is the bill?
Koliko je račun?

Please give me the bill.
Molim Vas dajte mi račun.

This bill is not correct.   *Please look the bill over.*
Ovaj račun nije točan.   **Molim Vas pregledajte račun.**

I want to go to the train station.
Želim ići na kolodvor.

...to the airport.
...na uzletište/aerodrom.

...the bus station.
...na autobusni kolodvor.

...to the dock.   *Please call a taxi for me.*
...do pristajališta.   **Molim Vas pozovite mi taksi.**

I hope that I can come again.
Nadam se da ću opet doći.

I shall be returning on September 2.
Vraćam se drugog rujna.

Can you book a room for that date?
Možete li rezervirati sobu za taj datum?

LAUNDRY

I would like to leave these clothes to be dry-cleaned.
Želim ostaviti ovu robu na kemijskom čišćenju.

...to be washed.　　　　　　　　　*...to be pressed.*
...za pranje.　　　　　　　　　　**...za glačanje.**

Can you get this stain out?
Možete li očistiti ovu mrlju?

It is coffee/wine/grease.
To je kava/vino/mast.

Can you repair this?
Možete li popraviti ovo?

Can you sew on a button?
Možete li prišiti dugme?

When will it be ready?
Kada će biti gotovo?

We want to wear them today.
Želimo ih obući danas.

It can be ready on Thursday.　　　*Day after tomorrow.*
Može biti gotovo u četvrtak.　　　**Preksutra.**

It will take two days.　　　　　　*Can it be sooner.*
Uzet će dva dana.　　　　　　　**Može li prije?**

Please wash these clothes.
Molim Vas operite ovo rublje.

We don't wash this kind of clothing.
Mi ne peremo takvo rublje.

AT THE BARBER SHOP

Where's the barber shop?
Gdje je brijačnica?

The barber shop is on the fourth floor.
Brijačnica je na četvrtom katu.

I would like a haircut.
Želim se ošišati.

Please give me a shave.
Molim Vas da me obrijete.

Please don't cut it too short.
Molim Vas nemojte odrezati prekratko.

Please cut a little more ...
Molim Vas odrežite malo više...

... off the front.	*...off the back.*
...s prijeda.	**...odzada.**
...off the sides	*...off the top.*
...sa strana.	**...odozgor.**

Please trim my moustache.
Molim Vas podrežite mi brkove.

Please trim my beard.
Molim Vas podrežite mi bradu.

That is just fine. Thank you.
To je dobro. Hvala.

How much?	*Thank you. I like it very much.*
Koliko?	**Hvala. Vrlo mi se sviđa.**

AT THE BEAUTY SALON

Is there a beauty salon in the hotel?
Ima li frizerski salon u hotelu?

Yes, there is.
Da, ima.

What floor?
Na kojem katu?

The fifth floor.
Na petom katu.

Can I make an appointment for tomorrow morning?
Mogu li ugovoriti vrijeme za sutra ujutro?

May I come this afternoon for a cut and blow dry?
Mogu li doći poslije podne na šišanje i fen frizuru?

What time? **U koliko sati?**	*Eleven o'clock.* **Jedanaest sati.**
I would like... **Ja želim...**	*...a haircut.* **...šišanje.**
...a trim. **....potkratiti kosu.**	*....a facial.* **...čišćenje lica.**
...a shampoo and set. **...pranje i frizuru.**	*...a permanent wave.* **...trajnu.**
...a manicure. **...maniker.**	*...a pedicure.* **...pediker.**
...a tint. **...bojanje.**	

...with bangs.
...sa šiškama.

...short.
...kratko.

...long.
...dugo.

...curly.
...kuštravo.

...straight.
...ravno.

...wavy.
...valovito.

...not too short.
...ne previše kratko.

Please don't use any hair spray.
Molim Vas nemojte upotrijebiti laka.

I want a darker color.
Želim tamniju boju.

...a lighter color.
...svijetliju boju.

...the same color.
...istu boju.

...chestnut color.
...kestenjastu boju.

...blonde.
...blondu boju.

...brunette.
...smeđu boju.

Thank you.
Hvala.

I like it.
Sviđa mi se.

CHANGING MONEY

All travellers need to familiarize themselves with the currency of the country that they are visiting. The following phrases will help you to exchange money in Croatia. You may obtain the most recent exchange rate and it will be helpful to familiarize yourself with the bills and coins before you leave home. It will also be useful to have a small amount of Croatian currency with you for immediate use upon your arrival.

Where is the [nearest] bank?
Gdje je [najbliža] banka?

The nearest currency office is on Savska Street.
Najbliža mjenjačnica je u Savskoj ulici.

Please write the address.
Molim Vas, napišite adresu.

What time does it open?
U koliko sati otvori?

It opens at nine.
Otvori u devet sati.

What time does it close?
U koliko zatvori?

It closes at five.
Zatvori u pet sati.

Is it open on Saturday?
Je li otvoreno subotom?

Yes, it is.
Da, je.

Where can I exchange American/Canadian dollars?
Gdje mogu promijeniti američke/kanadske dolare?

You can exchange money at the hotel.
Možete mijenjati novce u hotelu.

Is there an American Express office in the city?
Ima li American Express ured u ovom gradu?

I would like to cash this [traveller's] check.
Želim unovčiti ovaj [putnički] ček.

Can you cash this [personal] check?
Možete li unovčiti ovaj [osobni] ček?

Do you accept traveller's checks?
Primate li putničke čekove?

I want to change some money.
Želim promijeniti novce.

Please go to that window.
Molim Vas idite na onaj šalter.

I would like to change Australian dollars.
Želim promijeniti australske dolare.

...pounds.
...funte.

Your passport, please.
Vašu putovnicu, molim.

Here is my passport.
Evo moja putovnica.

How much will you change?
Koliko ćete promijeniti?

I want to change twenty dollars.
Želim promijeniti dvadeset dolara.

What is today's rate of exchange for the dollar?
Kakav je današnji tečaj za dolar?

What rate of commission do you charge?
Koliku uzimate proviziju?

Please give me some large bills and some small ones.
Molim Vas dajte mi velikih novčanica i nešto sitnih.

Here's the money.
Izvolite novce.

Please give me some smaller bills.
Molim Vas dajte mi manje novčanice.

Please count to see if it's right.
Molim Vas prebrojite da vidite ako je u redu.

Please sign here.
Molim Vas, potpišite ovdje.

Here is your receipt.
Evo Vam potvrda.

I have a letter of credit.
Imam akreditiv.

I'm expecting some money from Los Angeles.
Ja očekujem neke novce iz Los Angelesa.

Has it arrived yet?
Jesu li novci stigli?

Where should I sign?
Gdje trebam potpisati?

RESTAURANTS AND DINING

Croatians are a very hospitable people who enjoy entertaining and fine dining. Getting to know Croatians means getting to know the Croatian national cuisine. There is no greater honor than to serve one's guests a fine meal introduced by *šljivovica* and closing with a selection of delicate pastries. In addition to the phrases necessary to order your meals, we have included a menu reader of the most typical Croatian dishes prepared in all areas where Croatians live. *Dobar tek!*

What time shall we eat lunch/dinner?
U koliko sati ćemo ručati/večerati?

I'm hungry.
Ja sam gladan/gladna.

I'm thirsty.
Ja sam žedan/žedna.

Are you hungry?
Jeste li gladni?

Very hungry.
Vrlo gladan/gladna.

Are you thirsty?
Jeste li žedni?

I'm not hungry.
Nisam gladan/gladna.

I'm not thirsty.
Nisam žedan/žedna.

Do you want to eat now?
Želite li jesti sada?

Let's go eat now.
Hajdemo jesti sada.

Can you recommend a good, inexpensive restaurant?
Možete li preporučiti dobar, jeftin restoran?

Is there a restaurant at the hotel?
Ima li restoran u hotelu?

What floor is it on?
Na kojem je katu?

It's on the third floor.
Na trećem je katu.

Where shall we eat?
Gdje ćemo jesti?

Where is there a good restaurant?
Gdje ima dobar restoran?

What's it called?
Kako se zove?

It's called Šumski Dvor.
Zove se Šumski Dvor.

Is it far from here?
Je li daleko odavde?

No, it's very close.
Ne, vrlo je blizu.

What kind of restaurant is it?
Kakav je to restoran?

It is a restaurant that offers Croatian national specialities.
To je restoran koji nudi hrvatske domaće specijalitete.

It is a...
To je...

...seafood restaurant.
...riblji restoran.

...pizzeria.
...pizza restoran.

...vegetarian restaurant.
...vegeterijanski restoran.

...self-serve restaurant.
...express restoran.

...French restaurant.
...francuski restoran.

...Italian restaurant.
...talijanski restoran.

...a restaurant specializing in grilled lamb.
...restoran čiji je specijalitet pečena janjetina.

I would like to make a reservation.
Želim napraviti rezervaciju.

For how many people?
Za koliko osoba?

For eight.
Za osam.

What time are you coming?
U koliko sati dolazite?

We're coming at six.
Dolazimo u šest.

Do you have a table for three?
Imate li stol za troje?

Is there a table by the window/in a corner?
Ima li stol kraj prozora/u uglu?

We would like a table on the terrace.
Mi želimo stol na terasi.

You'll have to wait about fifteen minutes.
Morat ćete čekati oko petnaest minuta.

We don't serve lunch until 12:30.
Mi ne serviramo ručak do 12:30.

Dinner is not being served yet.
Večera se još ne servira.

We stop serving at midnight.
Mi prestajemo servirati u ponoć.

Where is the cloakroom?
Gdje je garderoba?

We are in a hurry.
Žuri nam se.

THE MEALS

Breakfast.
Doručak.

Lunch.
Ručak.

Dinner.
Večera.

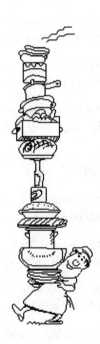

At what time is breakfast?
U koliko sati je doručak?

I want breakfast in my room.
Želim doručak u mojoj sobi.

Breakfast is served in the small restaurant.
Doručak se servira u malom restoranu.

AT THE TABLE

Where is the waiter?
Gdje je konobar?

Waiter, the menu please.
Konobaru, jelovnik molim.

Waiter, please bring an ashtray.
Konobaru, molim Vas donesite pepeonik.

What is the specialty of this restaurant?
Koji je specijalitet ovog restorana?

What do you recommend?
Što Vi preporučujete?

Please help us order.
Molim Vas pomozite nam naručiti.

Please bring the coffee now.
Molim Vas donesite kavu sada.

More butter, please.
Još maslaca, molim.

Bring some more sugar.
Donesite još šećera.

Bring me a glass of water, please.
Donesite mi čašu vode, molim Vas.

This coffee is cold.
Ova je kava hladna.

Do you take milk and sugar?
Uzimate li mlijeko i šećer?

Without sugar, please.
Bez šećera, molim Vas.

We eat only fruit at breakfast.
Mi jedemo samo voće za doručak.

This butter is not fresh.
Ovaj maslac nije svjež.

This milk is/is not warm.   *This milk is sour.*
Ovo mlijeko je/nije toplo.   Ovo je mlijeko prokislo.

I would like a glass of cold milk.
Želim čašu hladnog mlijeka.

Another cup of coffee?
Još jednu kavu?

Another cup of tea?
Još jedan čaj?

Do you want some more coffee?
Želite li još kave?

Nothing more, thank you.
Ništa više, hvala.

Would you like soup?
Želite li juhu?

Bring me a fork /knife/a spoon.   *This fork is dirty.*
Donesite mi vilicu/nož/žlicu.   Ova vilica je prljava.

This tablecloth is not clean.
Ovaj stolnjak nije čist.

Please bring me a napkin.
Molim Vas, donesite mi ubrus.

A glass of [ice] water.   *Please bring some ice.*
Cašu vode [s ledom].   **Molim Vas, donesite leda.**

What kind of wines do you have?
Kakva imate vina?

What kinds of liqueurs do you have?
Kakve imate likere?

A glass of beer.
Cašu piva.

Enjoy your meal!
Dobar tek!

Bottoms up!
Živili!

A bottle of white/red wine.
Bocu bijelog/crnog vina.

This is too hot (spicy).
Ovo je previše ljuto.

...sweet.	*...sour.*	*...salty.*	*...bitter.*
... slatko.	...kiselo.	...slano.	...gorko.

I didn't order this.
Ja ovo nisam naručio/naručila.

I'm allergic to...
Ja sam alergičan na...

I don't eat...
Ja ne jedem...

Do you eat fish?
Jedete li ribu?

He doesn't eat meat.
On ne jede meso.

I don't eat dessert.
Ja ne jedem poslastice.

He would like some ice cream.
On bi htio malo sladoleda.

Waiter, the check please.
Konobaru, račun molim.

How much do I owe you?
Koliko Vam dugujem?

Is the tip included?
Je li posluga uračunata?

Where do I pay?
Gdje se plaća?

At the cashier's booth.
Kod blagajne.

There's a mistake in the bill.
Ovaj račun nije točan.

Do you accept credit cards?
Primate li [kreditne] kartice?

May I pay with a traveller's check?
Mogu li platiti sa putničkim čekom?

I have already paid.
Ja sam već platio/platila.

RESTAURANT VOCABULARY

another chair	**drugu stolicu**	*pastry shop*	**slastičarna**
ashtray	**pepeonik**	*plate*	**tanjur**
bill	**račun**	*restaurant*	**restoran**
bowl	**zdjela**	*restroom*	**zahod**
café	**kavana**	*saucer*	**tanjurić**
cigarettes	**cigarete**	*service*	**usluga**
cloakroom	**garderoba**	*spoon*	**žlica**
course (dish)	**jelo**	*table*	**stol**
cup	**šalica**	*tablecloth*	**stolnjak**
fork	**vilica**	*terrace*	**terasa**
fresh	**svježe**	*thirsty*	**žedan**
glass	**čaša**	*tip*	**napojnica**
hungry	**gladan**	*toothpick*	**čačkalica**
knife	**nož**	*vegetarian*	**vegeterijanski**
main course	**glavno jelo**	*waiter*	**konobar**
matches	**žigice**	*waitress*	**konobarica**
menu	**jelovnik**	*washroom*	**zahod**
napkin	**ubrus**	*wine & spirits*	**alkoholna pića**

FOOD AND DRINK

aperitif	**aperitif**	*cognac*	**konjak**
appetizer	**predjelo**	*cordial*	**slatki liker**
apple juice	**sok od jabuke**	*dessert*	**poslastica**
beer	**pivo**	*espresso*	**espresso**
brandy	**vinjak/rakija**	*fish*	**riba**
bread	**kruh**	*french-fries*	**pržen krumpir/**
butter	**maslac**		**pomfrit**
cheese	**sir**	*fruit*	**voće**
cider	**jabukovac**	*(fruit) juice*	**(voćni) sok**
(hot) chocolate	**kakao**	*game*	**divljač**
coffee	**kava**	*gin*	**džin**
with cream	**sa šlagom**	*gin and tonic*	**džin tonik**

grapefruit juice	sok od grepfruta	salt	sol
ice cream	sladoled	sandwich	sendvič
ketchup	kečup	Scotch whiskey	škotski viski
lemon	limun	sherry	šeri
lemonade	limunada	seafood	morski
liqueur	liker		specijaliteti
meat	meso	seasoning	začin
milk	mlijeko	soup	juha
mineral water	mineralna voda	starter	predjelo
mustard	senf	sugar	šećer
olive oil	maslinovo ulje	tea	čaj
orange juice	sok od naranče	with lemon	s limunom
pepper	papar	with rum	s rumom
pineapple juice	sok od ananasa	tomato juice	sok od rajčica
port wine	port vino	tonic water	tonik
potato	krumpir	vegetables	povrće
poultry	perad	vinegar	ocat
red wine	crno vino	vodka	votka
rice	riža	(ice) water	voda (s ledom)
rolls	zemičke	wine	vino
rum	rum	wine list	vinska karta
saccharine	saharin	whiskey	viski
salad	salata	white wine	bijelo vino

HOW FOODS MAY BE PREPARED

baked	pečeno	ground/mined	mljeveno
barbecued	na gradele/	overcooked	prekuhano
	na ražnju/	pickled	kiselo
	na žaru	roasted	pečeno
boiled	kuhano	smoked	dimljeno
braised	pirjano	steamed	kuhano na
breaded	pohano		pari
fried	prženo	stewed	pirjano
grilled	na gradele/	stuffed	punjeno
	na roštilju/	sunny side up	na oko
	na žaru	uncooked	svježe
marinated	marinirano	with a sauce	s umakom
mixed	mješano		

READING THE MENU

ananas	pineapple	divljač	game
badem	almond	dunja	quince
bakalar	codfish	džem	jam
barbun	red mullet	đuveč	Croatian
bečki odrezak	Wiener Schnitzel		baked casserole
biftek	beefsteak	fazan	pheasant
bijeli luk	garlic	fažol	dried beans
bijelica	whitefish	file	fillet
bijelo meso	breast (poultry)	fileki	tripe
blitva	Swiss chard	gemišt	wine with
borovnice	blueberries		mineral water
		girice	smelts
bosanski lonac	Bosnian	gljive	mushrooms
	casserole	govedina	beef
brancin	sea-bass	goveđa juha	clear beef soup
breskve	peaches	grah	beans
brodet	Dalmatian fish	grašak	peas
	stew	grožđe	grapes
bubrežnjak	tenderloin	grožđice	raisins
burek	meat or cheese	gulaš	goulash
	strudel	guska	goose
but	leg of	hladetina	pork in aspic
cikla	beet	hladno	cold
cipal	grey mullet	hobotnica	octopus
cvjetača	cauliflower	hren	horseradish
čaj	tea	hrenovka	hot dog
s limunom	with lemon	ikra	caviar
s rumom	with rum	iverak	flounder
češnjak	garlic	jabuka	apple
čokolada	chocolate	janjetina	lamb
čvarci	cracklings	jagode	strawberries
ćevapčići	barbecued meat	jaja	eggs
	rolls	jegulje	eel
đagnje	mussels	jesetra	sturgeon
dinja	melon	jastog	lobster
		jetra	liver

junetina	baby beef	lonac	casserole
kalamari	squid	losos	salmon
kamenice	oysters	lozovača	grape brandy
karmenadla	pork loin roast	lubenica	watermelon
kavijar	caviar	lubin	sea bass
kečiga	sterlet	luk	onion
keksi	biscuits (cookies)	lješnjaci	hazelnuts
		mahune	string beans
kesten	chestnut	majoneza	mayonnaise
kiflice	croissants	mak	poppy seeds
kisela voda	mineral water	makovnjača	poppy seed roll (cake)
kiselo mlijeko	buttermilk		
kobasice	sausages	maline	raspberries
komovica	grape brandy	manestra	pasta dish
kompot	stewed fruit	marelice	apricots
kopar	dill	marmelada	jam
kotlovina	grilled meat specialty	maslac	butter
		masline	olives
kotlet	chop	med	honey
kolači	cakes & cookies	medenjaci	honey cookies
		meso	meat
kovač	John Dory fish	mješano	mixed
		mladica	trout
krastavac	cucumber	mrkva	carrots
krema	cream pudding	mušule	mussels
		na gradele	grilled
krempita	cream slice	na roštilju	grilled
krumpir	potato	na ražnju	barbecued on a spit
kruška	pear		
krvavica	blood sausage	na maslacu	in butter
kuhano	boiled	na ulju	in oil
kunić	rabbit	nabujak	soufflé
kupus	cabbage	nar	pomegranate
lešo	boiled	naranča	orange
lignje	squid	naravni odrezak	plain veal cutlet
limun	lemon	odojak	suckling pig
list	sole		

odrezak	cutlet
okruglice	dumplings
orada	bream
orasi	walnuts
orehnjača	walnut roll
oslić	hake
ovčetina	mutton
palačinke	Croatian crêpes
paprika	bell pepper
paprika	paprika
pastrva	trout
pašteta	paté
pašticada	Dalmatian pot roast
patka	duck
pecivo	bun, roll
pečenje	roast
pečurke	mushrooms
pekmez	plum jam
perkelt	type of stew
peršun	parsley
pileća juha	chicken soup
pire	purée
piletina	chicken
pirjano	braised
pita	Croatian pie
pladanj	platter
pljeskavica	hamburger steak
pogačice	biscuits
pohano	breaded
polpete	meatballs
pomfrit	french fries
poriluk	leek
poslastice	dessert

povrće	vegetables
prepržen kruh	toast
prokule	brussels sprouts
prstaci	mussels
pršut	Dalmatian ham
prženo	fried
račići	shrimp
ragu	stew
rajčica	tomato
rak	crab
rakija	brandy
ratluk	Turkish delight
raženi kruh	rye bread
ražnjići	kebobs
rebra	ribs
rezanci	noodles
riba	fish
ričet	rice & barley dish
riža	rice
rižoto	risotto
rolada	roll
ružmarin	rosemary
salama	salami
salata	salad
sarma	stuffed cabbage rolls
sardela	anchovy
savijača	strudel
sendvič	sandwich
sipa	cuttlefish
sir	cheese
skuša	mackerel
sladoled	ice cream
slanina	bacon
smokve	figs
smuđ	perch

snijeg	meringue	šunka	ham
svinjetina	pork	teletina	veal
som	catfish	toplo	warm
srnetina	venison	torta	torte (cake)
šampinjoni	mushrooms	trešnje	cherries
šaran	carp	tučeno vrhnje	whipped cream
šato	wine sauce		
šipak	rose hip	tunina	tuna
škampi	prawns	umak	sauce
šlag	whipped cream	vanilice	vanilla crescents
šljive	plums	vinjak	wine brandy
šnicle	cutlets	višnje	sour cherries
šljivovica	plum brandy	voćna salata	fruit salad
špagete	spaghetti	vrganji	boletus mushrooms
šparoga	asparagus		
štruklji	salty cheese strudel	vrhnje	cream
		zelje	cabbage
štuka	pike	zelena salata	lettuce salad
školjke	shellfish	zubatac	dentex (fish)
špinat	spinach		

SHOPPING

Shopping in a foreign country can be a real adventure, but it is ever so much more enjoyable when you can make yourself easily understood. Included in this section are typical questions and answers that will be useful for shopping trips in Croatia. Since weights and sizes are different, we have also included conversion tables for your convenience.

Where is the best...?
Gdje je najbolji...?

Where is the nearest...?
Gdje je najbliži...?

Where can I buy...?
Gdje mogu kupiti...?

Where is the market?
Gdje je tržnica?

I would like to buy...
Želim kupiti...

At what time do the stores open/close?
U koliko se sati otvore/zatvore trgovine?

Can you recommend a...?
Možete li preporučiti...?

STORES AND SHOPS

antique store	antikvarijat	*grocery*	supermarket
art gallery	galerija umjetnosti	*hardware store*	željezara
		hospital	bolnica
bakery	pekara	*jeweller*	zlatar
bank	banka	*laundry*	praonica
barber	brijačnica	*market*	tržnica
beauty salon	frizerski salon	*newsstand*	kiosk za prodaju novina
book store	knjižara		
butcher	mesar	*optician*	optičar
camera store	trgovina za fotoaparate	*pastry shop*	slastičarna
		pharmacy	ljekarna
candy store	trgovina bombona	*photoshop*	trgovina za fotografsku opremu
chemist	ljekarna		
dairy	mljekarna	*police station*	policijska uspostava
dentist	stomatolog, zubar		
		post office	pošta
department store	robna kuća	*shoe repair shop*	postolarska radnja
doctor	liječnik	*shoe shop*	trgovina cipela
dressmaker	šivačica	*souvenir shop*	trgovina suvenira
drug store	ljekarna	*sporting goods shop*	trgovina sportske opreme
dry cleaner	kemijska čistionica		
		stationer	papirnica
filling station	benzinska postaja	*supermarket*	supermarket
		tailor	krojač
florist	cvjećarnica	*toiletry shop*	trgovina kozmetike
food store	supermarket		
gas station	benzinska postaja	*travel agency*	putna agencija
		watchmaker	urar

AT THE STORE

Please help me.
Molim Vas pomozite mi.

Are you a salesperson?
Jeste li Vi prodavač(ica)?

What do you wish to buy?
Što želite kupiti?

Do you have...?
Imate li...?

Please show me some.....
Molim Vas pokažite mi...

What size, please?
Koji broj, molim Vas?

Try on these....
Probajte ove....

May I help you?
Izvolite.

I would like...
Želio/željela bih...

I would like to buy....
Želim kupiti....

How much does that cost?
Koliko to stoji?

How much do they cost?
Koliko stoje?

That is too much.
To je previše.

That is cheap.
To je jeftino.

I (don't) like this.
Ovo mi se (ne) sviđa.

I will take this.
Ja ću uzeti ovo.

This is the wrong size.
Ovo je krivi broj.

This dress is too short.
Ova je haljina prekratka.

Please show me ...
Molim Vas pokažite mi...

...another.
...drugi.

...a larger size.
... veći broj.

...a smaller size.
...manji broj.

...a cheaper one.
...jeftiniji.

This skirt is too long.
Ova je suknja predugačka.

I would like to see a white shirt.
Želim vidjeti bijelu košulju.

I don't like this color.
Meni se ne sviđa ova boja.

Have you a lighter/darker blue dress?
Imate li svjetliju/tamniju plavu haljinu?

I like the one in the window.
Sviđa mi se onaj/ona u izlogu.

I like the style, but not the color.
Sviđa mi se kroj, ali ne boja.

The sleeves are too wide.
Rukavi su preširoki.

The sleeves are too narrow.
Rukavi su preuski.

I would like to try on some shoes.
Želim probati cipele.

A pair of black (brown) shoes.
Par crnih (smeđih) cipela.

Try this pair on.
Probajte ovaj par.

These are too narrow.	*They are too tight /loose.*
Ove su preuske.	**Pretijesne/preširoke su.**

They are not big enough.	*They are too long/short.*
Nisu dovoljno velike.	**Predugačke/prekratke su.**

I want to buy needles, pins and some thread.
Želim kupiti igle, pribadačice i malo konca.

Is this made in Croatia?	*Is this hand-made?*
Je li to hrvatski proizvod?	**Je li to ručni rad?**

No, it is machine-made.
Ne, to je strojni proizvod.

What is it made of?
Od čega je to napravljeno?

Is is made of...
To je od...

...cotton	...wool	...silk	...rayon
...pamuka	**...vune**	**...svile**	**...viskoze**

....linen	...leather	...glass	...crystal
...lana	**...kože**	**...stakla**	**...kristala**

....brass	...bronze	...silver	...gold
...mjeda	**...bronca**	**...srebra**	**...zlata**

Is this one alright?	*I'll show you another.*
Je li ovaj u redu?	**Pokazat ću Vam drugi.**

We don't have any...
Nemamo...

How many do you want to buy?
Koliko želite kupiti?

Just one, thank you.
Samo jedan, hvala.

Three, please.
Tri, molim Vas.

Anything else?
Još nešto?

No, thank you. That's all.
Ne, hvala. To je sve.

I'll take it (them) with me.
Uzet ću ga/je (ih) sa sobom.

Will you wrap it, please?
Umotajte ga/je, molim Vas.

Send it to my hotel, please.
Pošaljite u moj hotel, molim Vas.

Please send it to this address.
Molim Vas pošaljite na ovu adresu.

Pack it (them) for shipment to....
Zapakujte za prijevoz u ...

How much altogether?
Koliko sveukupno?

Here is the bill.
Evo račun.

Is there a discount?
Ima li popusta?

Do you take credit cards?
Primate li [kreditne] kartice?

May I pay with an American Express/Visa card?
Mogu li platiti sa karticom American Express/Visa?

We [do not] accept credit cards.
[Ne] primamo kreditne kartice.

Do you accept dollars?
Primate li dolare?

I will pay cash.
Platit ću u gotovini.

The cashier is over there.
Blagajna je tamo.

I bought this yesterday.
Kupio/kupila sam ovo jučer.

It doesn't work/fit.
Ne radi/ne odgovara.

I would like to exhange it.
Želim ga zamijeniti.

May I speak with the manager?
Mogu li govoriti s direktorom?

I don't want to buy anything.
Ne želim ništa kupiti.

I'm just looking.
Samo gledam.

You have a nice shop/boutique.
Imate lijep dučan/butik.

Please come again.
Dođite nam opet.

PHARMACEUTICALS AND TOILETRIES

aspirin	aspirin	Kleenex	papirnate maramice
after-shave lotion	losion za brijanje	laxative	laksativ
baby cream	krema za bebe	lip gloss	sjaj za usne
baby powder	puder za bebe	lip pencil	krejon za usne
band-aids	flasteri	lipstick	ruž za usne
cotton	vata	lipstick brush	četkica za usne
cough drops	bomboni za kašalj	make-up bag	torbica za šminku
cough syrup	sirup za kašalj	make-up	šminka
deodorant	dezoderans	make-up remover	mlijeko za skidanje šminke
diapers	pelene		
ear drops	kapi za uši	mascara	maskara
emery board	šmirgla za nokte	moisturizing cream	hidrantna krema
eye drops	kapi za oči	nail brush	četkica za nokte
eye liner	ajlajner	nail clippers	noktorezac
eye pencil	olovka za obrve	nail file	turpija za nokte
eye shadow	sjenilo za oči	nail polish	lak za nokte
face powder	puder za lice	nail polish remover	aceton
first-aid kit	pribor za prvu pomoć	nail scissors	škarice za nokte
foot cream	krema za noge		
hand cream	krema za ruke	perfume	parfem
hair brush	četka za kosu	razor	brijač
hair gel	gel za kosu	rouge	rumenilo
hair mousse	pjena za kosu	safety pins	ziherice
hair net	mreža za kosu	sanitary napkins	higijenski uložci
hair pins	ukosnice		
hair spray	lak za kosu	sedative	sedativ
hair wig	perika	shampoo	šampon
insect repellent	sredstvo za zaštitu od kukaca	shaving brush	četka za brijanje
iodine	jod	shaving cream	krema za brijanje

shaving soap	**sapun za brijanje**	*tissues*	**papirnate maramice**
sleeping pills	**pilule za spavanje**	*toilet paper*	**toaletni papir**
soap	**sapun**	*toothbrush*	**četkica za zube**
suntan lotion	**losion za sunčanje**	*toothpaste*	**pasta za zube**
suntan oil	**ulje za sunčanje**	*towel*	**ručnik**
talcum powder	**talk**	*tranquilizers*	**umirujuća sredstva**
tampons	**tamponi**	*tweezers*	**pinceta**
thermometer	**termometar**	*vitamin pills*	**vitamini**
throat lozenges	**bomboni za kašalj**	*washcloth*	**krpica za lice**

THE CAMERA SHOP AND APPLIANCE STORE

How much would it cost to process this film?
Koliko bi došlo razviti ovaj film?

When will it be ready?
Kada će biti gotovo?

I'd like to buy film for this camera.
Želim kupiti film za ovaj aparat.

I want two prints of each negative.
Želim dvije slike od svakog negativa.

This camera is broken. Can you repair it?
Ovaj aparat ne radi. Možete li ga popraviti?

Something is wrong with the...
Nešto nije u redu sa...

...automatic lens.
...automatskim objektivom.

...shutter.
...blendom.

...range-finder.
...daljinarom.

...film feed.
...pomicanjem filma.

...exposure meter.
...svjetlomjerom.

battery	**baterija**	*flash*	**blic**
black & white film	**crno-bijeli film**	*hair dryer*	**fen za kosu**
		iron	**glačalo**
camera	**foto-aparat**	*lens*	**objektiv**
cassette	**kazeta**	*light meter*	**svjetlomjer**
cassette player	**kazetofon**	*plug*	**utikač**
clock	**sat**	*radio*	**radio**
color film	**film u boji**	*razor*	**brijač**
color slides	**dijapozitivi u boji**	*record*	**ploča**
		tape recorder	**magnetofon**
fast film	**brzi film**	*television*	**televizor**
film	**film**	*transformer*	**transformator**
filter	**filtar**	*tripod*	**tronožac**

SMOKING TERMS

carton of cigarettes	**karton cigareta**	*lighter fluid*	**tekučina za upaljač**
cigarette paper	**papir za cigarete**	*matches*	**žigice**
		menthol	**mentol**
cigarettes	**cigarete**	*pack of cigarettes*	**paket cigareta**
cigars	**cigare**		
filtered	**s filtarom**	*pipe*	**lula**
lighter	**upaljač**	*tobacco*	**duhan**
		without filter	**bez filtera**

BOOKS AND STATIONERY

address book	**adresar**	*computer diskettes*	**diskete za računalo**
ball-point pen	**penkala**		
book	**knjiga**	*dictionary*	**rječnik**
cellophane tape	**celofan**	*pocket dictionary*	**džepni rječnik**

envelopes	omotnice	*pencil*	šiljilo
exercise book	teka	*sharpener*	
file folder	faksikl	*playing cards*	karte
fountain pen	naliv-pero	*postcards*	razglednice
glue	ljepilo	*ruler*	mjerilo
grammar book	gramatika	*sketching pad*	papir za
guide-book	vodič (knjiga)		crtanje
ink	tinta	*string*	špaga
labels	naljepnice	*tissue paper*	svileni papir
magazine	časopis	*tissues*	papirne
map	karta		maramice
city map	plan grada	*typewriter*	vrpca za pisaći
road map	putna karta	*ribbon*	stroj
newspapers	novine	*typing paper*	papir za
American	američke		tipkanje
English	engleske	*wrapping paper*	papir za
notebook	bilježnica		umotavanje
pen	penkala	*writing paper*	papir za
pencil	olovka		pisanje

SOUVENIRS

ashtray	pepeonik	*leather goods*	kožni proizvodi
bracelet	narukvica	*manicure set*	pribor za
brooch	broš		manikiranje
ceramics	keramika	*necklace*	ogrlica
chain	lančić	*painting*	slika
crystal	kristal	*pendant*	privjesak
cuff-links	dugmad za	*pin*	broš
	manšete	*pocket knife*	džepni nož
cutlery	jedaći pribor	*ring*	prsten
earrings	naušnice	*rugs*	tepisi
furs	krzno	*silver*	srebro
glass	staklo	*statue*	kip
handbag	torba	*wallet*	novčarka
handicrafts	rukotvorine	*watch*	sat
jewelry	dragulji		

Clothing

apron	pregača
bathing suit	kupaći kostim
bath robe	kupaći kaput
bath towel	ručnik za kupanje
belt	remen
blazer	sako
blouse	bluza
bow tie	leptir mašna
bra	grudnjak
briefs	gačice
buckle	kopča za remen
button	dugme
cardigan	vesta/ džemper
checked	karirano
chiffon	šifon
coat	kaput
collar	ovratnik
corduroy	kordsamt
cotton	pamuk
cuffs	manšete
denim	traper
dress	haljina
dressing gown	kući ogrtač
evening gown	večernja haljina
flannel	flanel
fur coat	krzneni kaput
gabardine	gabarden
gloves	rukavice
handkerchief	maramica
hat	šešir
hem	porub
houndstooth	pepita

jeans	traperice
lace	čipka
lapel	suvratak
leather	koža
linen	lan
lining	podstava
nylon	najlon
overcoat	ogrtač
panties	gačice
panty hose	hulahopke
pocket	džep
polka-dotted	na točke
pullover	pulover
pyjamas	pidžama
raincoat	kišna kabanica
rayon	viskoza
ribbon	traka
satin	saten
rubber boots	gumene čizme
sandals	sandale
shirt	košulja
shoes	cipele
shorts	kratke hlače
silk	svila
skirt	suknja
sleeve	rukav
slip	podsuknja
slippers	papuče
socks	kratke čarape
solid color	solidne boje
sports jacket	sportski sako
stockings	čarape
striped	prugast
suit (men's)	odijelo
suit (women's)	kostim
suede	antilop
sweater	džemper

T-shirt	**majica**	*underpants*	**gaće**
tennis shoes	**tenisice**	*undershirt*	**podkošulja**
tie	**kravata**	*velvet*	**samt**
tights	**hulahopke**	*vest*	**prsluk**
track suit	**trenirka**	*waistcoat*	**prsluk**
trousers	**hlače**	*wool*	**vuna**
umbrella	**kišobran**	*zipper*	**patentni zatvarač**

Colors

beige	**bež**	*mauve*	**svjetloljubičast**
blue	**plavo**	*orange*	**narančast**
brown	**smeđe**	*pink*	**roza**
cream	**krem**	*purple*	**ljubičast**
fawn	**žućkasto smeđe**	*red*	**crven**
gold	**zlatan**	*silver*	**srebren**
green	**zelen**	*turquoise*	**tirkiz**
grey	**siv**	*white*	**bijel**
		yellow	**žut**

Clothing Sizes: Ladies

Dresses and Suits							
American	8	10	12	14	16	18	20
British	30	32	34	36	38	40	42
Continental	34	36	38	40	42	44	46

Sweaters							
American	34	36	38	40	42	44	46
British	36	38	40	42	44	46	48
Continental	42	44	46	48	50	52	54

Stockings							
Am. & Br.	8	8½	9	9½	10	10½	11
Continental	35	36	37	38	39	40	41

Shoes								
American	6	6½	7	7½	8	8½	9	10
British	4½	5	5½	6	6½	7	7½	8½
Continental	36	37	38	38	39	39	40	42

Clothing Sizes: Men

Suits, Jackets & Overcoats						
Am. & Br.	34	36	38	40	42	44	46
Continental	44	46	48	50	52	54	56

Shirts						
Am. & Br.	14½	15	15½	16	16½	17
Continental	37	38	39	40	41	42

Socks						
Am. & Br.	9½	10	10½	11	11½	12	12½
Continental	39	40	41	42	43	44	45

Shoes						
American	8½	9	9½	10	10½	11	11½
British	8	8½	9	9½	10	10½	11
Continental	42	43	43	44	44	45	45

PROVISIONS

Listed below are some of the foods and accessories that you might take on a picnic or on a camping trip.

apples	**jabuke**	*coffee*	**kava**
bananas	**banane**	*cold cuts*	**hladni narezci**
biscuits	**keks**	*cookies*	**kolači**
bottle		*corkscrew*	**vadičep**
opener	**otvarač boca**	*crackers*	**slani keks**
box of...	**kutija...**	*cream*	**vrhnje**
bread	**kruh**	*cucumbers*	**krastavci**
butter	**maslac**	*eggs*	**jaja**
cakes	**kolači**	*flour*	**brašno**
candy	**bomboni**	*frankfurters*	**kobasice**
can of...	**konzerva...**	*ham*	**šunka, pršut**
cheese	**sir**	*ice-cream*	**sladoled**
chocolate	**čokolada**	*lemonade*	**limunada**

lemons	**limuni**	*potatoes*	**krumpiri**
lettuce	**zelena salata**	*rolls*	**pecivo**
milk	**mlijeko**	*salad*	**salata**
mustard	**senf**	*salami*	**salama**
noodles	**rezanci**	*salt*	**sol**
oranges	**naranče**	*sandwiches*	**sendviči**
package of...	**paket...**	*sausage*	**kobasice**
pepper	**papar**	*sugar*	**šećer**
peppers	**paprike**	*sweets*	**slatkiši**
pickles	**kiseli krastavci**	*tea*	**čaj**
potato chips	**čips**	*tomatoes*	**rajčice**

Weights and Measures

Weights

1 kilo(gram) [kg.] = 1,000 grams [g.]

100 g. = 3.5 oz.	½ kg. = 1 lb. 1.5 oz.
200 g. = 7 oz.	1 kg. = 2 lb. 3 oz.

1 oz. = 28.36 g.

1 lb. = 453.6 g.

Liquid Measures

1 liter (l.) = .88 Imp. quart = 1.06 U.S. quart

1 imperial quart. = 1.14 l.	1 U.S. quart = 0.95 l.
1 imperial gal. = 4.55 l.	1 U.S. gal. = 3.8 l.

GETTING AROUND BY AUTOMOBILE

You may not find too many attendants at gas stations and repair shops who speak English, so speaking some Croatian will be very helpful. The following phrases will help you to purchase gasoline and supplies, get directions and if necessary, to get some help should you get lost or if you run into car problems.

I would like to rent a car.
Želim iznajmiti auto.

How much does a car cost per day/per week?
Koliko stoji auto na dan/na tjedan?

Is the mileage included?
Je li uračunata kilometraža?

How much per kilometer?
Koliko po kilometru?

Is a deposit needed?
Treba li kaucija?

Is gasoline expensive in Croatia?
Jeli benzin skup u Hrvatskoj?

I want a car with seatbelts and an outside mirror.
Hoću auto sa sigurnosnim pojasima i retrovizorom.

I will/will not take the car out of Croatia.
Ja ću/neću voziti auto izvan Hrvatske.

I want to leave it in Osijek.
Želim ga ostaviti u Osijeku.

How much is the insurance per day?
Koliko stoji osiguranje na dan?

Here is the registration and the key.
Evo Vam registracija i ključ.

Where is the gas station?
Gdje je benzinska postaja?

*...a garage (*auto repair shop*)?*
...servisna radiona?

AT THE SERVICE STATION

Fill it up, please.
Napunite, molim Vas.

Give me twenty liters of gasoline.
Dajte mi dvadeset litara benzina.

The oil needs changing.
Treba promijeniti ulje.

Please check the tire pressure.
Molim Vas provjerite zrak u gumama.

Please add some water.
Molim Vas dodajte vode.

Please clean the windshield.
Molim Vas operite vjetrobran.

Wash the car, please.
Operite auto, molim Vas.

Please check the water/battery.
Molim Vas, pregledajte vodu/akumulator.

The tire is punctured.
Guma je probušena.

Can you fix a flat tire?
Možete li popraviti probušenu gumu?

The car won't start.
Auto neće upaliti.

The engine is overheating.
Pregrijava se motor.

The battery is dead. It needs to be charged.
Akumulator je prazan. Treba ga napuniti.

I don't know what the problem is.
Neznam kakav je kvar.

Is there a mechanic here?
Ima li mehaničara ovdje?

How much will you charge?
Koliko ćete naplatiti?

Can you fix it right away?
Možete li popraviti odmah?

How long will it take?
Koliko će dugo uzeti?

I need it as soon as possible.
Treba mi što prije.

It will be ready at 3.
Bit će gotovo u tri.

Your car is ready.
Vaš auto je gotov.

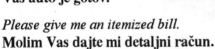

Please give me an itemized bill.
Molim Vas dajte mi detaljni račun.

Have you a map of the city?
Imate li kartu grada?

Can I buy a map of Croatia?
Mogu li kupiti kartu Hrvatske?

Where does this road lead to?   *Is this the road to Split?*
Kuda vodi ova cesta?   **Ide li ova cesta za Split?**

Is the road good?
Je li cesta dobra?

It is...
To je...

...a narrow road.
...uska cesta.

...a wide road.	... a bad road.	...a narrow bridge.
...široka cesta.	...loša cesta.	...uski most.

Is there a speed limit ?
Je li brzina ograničena?

You were driving too fast.
Vozili ste prebrzo.

You must pay the fine.
Morate platiti kaznu.

I'm sorry, officer.
Žalim, gospodine.

I didn't see the sign/light.
Nisam vidio/vidjela natpis/semafor.

Your driver's license, please.
Vozačku iskaznicu, molim Vas.

I have an international driver's license.
Ja imam međunarodnu vozačku iskaznicu.

Is this your car?
Je li ovo Vaš auto?

Please show me the registration.
Molim Vas pokažite mi registraciju.

ACCIDENTS

Please call the police.
Molim Vas zovite policiju.

There's been an accident.
Dogodila se nesreća.

It's about a kilometer from...
Otprilike kilometar od...

Would you please act as a witness?
Molim Vas budite svjedok.

Is anyone hurt?
Je li itko povrijeđen?

Don't move.
Nemojte se micati.

It's all right. Don't worry.
Sve je u redu. Nemojte brinuti.

Call an ambulance immediately.
Odmah zovite kola hitne pomoći.

There are people hurt.
Ima provrijeđenih osoba.

ASKING THE WAY

Excuse me, can you tell me where is...?
Oprostite, možete li mi reći gdje je...?

Is this the way to...?
Je li ovo put za...?

Which is the road for...?
Koja je cesta za...?

Please tell me where I am.
Molim Vas recite mi gdje sam.

How far is the city from here?
Koliko je grad daleko odavde?

Please tell me how to get to...
Molim Vas recite mi kako doći do...

I'm looking for...
Ja tražim...

We want to go by highway to...
Želimo ići autoputom do...

What is the best route to...?
Koji je najbolji put za...?

Is there a scenic route to...?
Ima li slikovit put do... ?

Where does this road lead?
Kuda vodi ova cesta?

Will we get to the city by evening?
Hoćemo li stići do grada dovečer?

Please show me on the map.
Molim Vas pokažite mi na putnoj karti.

Where's the nearest restaurant?
Gdje je najbliži restoran?

DIRECTIONS

Take that road.
Idite tom cestom.

Go straight ahead.
Idite ravno.

There.
Tamo.

Turn right.
Skrenite desno.

Turn left.
Skrenite lijevo.

Keep right.
Držite se desno.

Keep left.
Držite se lijevo.

Follow this road for 10 kilometers.
Idite ovom cestom 10 kilometara.

Turn left at the crossroads.
Skrenite lijevo na raskrsnici.

Turn right at the traffic light.
Skrenite desno na semaforu.

Turn right after the bridge.
Skrenite desno poslije mosta.

Take this road to...then ask again.
Idite ovom cestom do...onda pitajte ponovo.

May I park here?
Mogu li parkirati ovdje?

AUTOMOTIVE TERMS

accelerator	**pedala gasa**	*cylinder*	**cilindar**
air conditioning	**klimatizacija**	*distilled water*	**destilirana**
air filter	**filtar za zrak**		**voda**
alternator	**alternator**	*distributor*	**razvodnik**
anti-freeze	**antifriz**	*door*	**vrata**
axle	**osovina**	*drive (to)*	**voziti**
battery	**akumulator**	*driver*	**vozač**
brakes	**kočnice**	*dynamo*	**dinamo**
carburetor	**karburator/ rasplinjač**	*electrical system*	**električni sistem**
condenser	**kondenzator**	*engine*	**motor**
choke	**čok**	*exhaust*	**ispušna cijev**
clutch	**kvačilo**	*fan*	**ventilator**
cooling system	**hlađenje**	*fan belt*	**remen**
crankshaft	**radilica**		**ventilatora**

English	Croatian	English	Croatian
filter (air)	**filtar (za zrak)**	*roof-rack*	**krovni prtljažnik**
filter (oil)	**filtar (za ulje)**		
fuse	**osigurač**	*seat*	**sjedalo**
gearbox	**mjenjač**	*seatbelt*	**sigurnosni pojas**
generator	**generator**		
headlight	**prednje svjetlo**	*shock absorber*	**amortizer**
heater	**grijač**	*spare tire*	**rezervna guma**
heating	**grijanje**		
hood	**poklopac**	*spark plug*	**svjećica**
horn	**truba**	*speed*	**brzina**
hose	**cijev**	*speedometer*	**brzinomjer**
ignition system	**paljenje**	*stalling*	**motor se gasi**
jack	**dizalica**	*(the motor stalls)*	
lights	**žarulje**	*starter*	**pokretač**
mechanical trouble	**kvar na autu**	*steering wheel*	**upravljač**
mirror	**zrcalo**	*suspension*	**opruge kotača**
muffler	**prigušivač**	*tank*	**rezervoar**
oil	**ulje**	*tire*	**guma**
oil pressure	**pritisak ulja**	*tire pressure*	**pritisak u gumama**
overdrive	**peta brzina**		
points	**platine**	*transmission*	**transmisija**
radiator	**hladnjak**	*turn signal*	**žmigavac**
reverse gear	**brzina za vožnju unazad**	*wheels*	**kotači**
		window	**prozor**
		wipers	**brisači**

Fluid Measures

liters	imp. gals.	U.S. gals.	liters	imp. gals.	U.S. gals.
5	1.1	1.3	30	6.6	7.8
10	2.2	2.6	35	7.7	9.1
15	3.3	3.9	40	8.8	10.4
20	4.4	5.2	45	9.9	11.7
25	5.5	6.5	50	11	13

Tire Pressure

lbs/ in.^{2}	kg./cm.^{2}	lbs/ in.^{2}	kg./cm.^{2}
10	0.7	27	1.9
12	0.8	28	2.0
15	1.1	30	2.1
18	1.3	33	2.3
20	1.4	35	2.5
21	1.5	38	2.7
23	1.6	40	2.8
24	1.7	42	2.9
26	1.8	44	3.0

Miles into Kilometers

miles	10	20	30	40	50	60	70	80	90	100
kilometers	16	32	50	65	80	100	115	130	145	160

Kilometers into Miles

kilometers	10	25	40	50	60	80	90	100	120	130
miles	6	15	25	30	35	50	55	60	75	80

CROATIAN AND INTERNATIONAL ROAD SIGNS

For automotive signs and symbols please refer to the general section on signs and symbols.

GETTING AROUND BY TAXI, BUS AND TRAM

You will find clearly marked taxis at ranks in all the major towns and tourist centers in Croatia. They will have meters, but in smaller places, where there may be only one or two taxis, you will have to ask the fare in advance. There may be extra charges for luggage and night travel. Travel by bus or tram is inexpensive and will give you an opportunity to use the phrases that you have learned so far. The following phrases should get you through most situations travelling by taxi, bus or tram.

TAXI

Call a taxi, please.
Molim Vas pozovite taksi.

Please help me call a taxi.
Molim Vas pomozite mi pozvati taksi.

Please write it down. I want to show the driver.
Molim Vas napišite to. Želim pokazati vozaču.

Are you free?
Jeste li slobodni?

How much do you charge by the hour/per day?
Koliko računate na sat/na dan?

I want to go to... How much would you charge?
Hoću ići do... Koliko biste računali?

I don't want to pay that much.   *That is too much.*
Ne želim platiti toliko.   **To je previše.**

Where to, sir?
Kamo, gospodine?

*I want to go here. (*Giving driver address*)*
Želim ići ovamo.

Please take me to the American Embassy.
Molim Vas odvezite me do američke ambasade.

Put my luggage into the taxi.
Stavite moju prtljagu u taksi.

Drive to the railroad station/airport.
Vozite do željezničkog kolodvora/uzletišta.

Please hurry. I'm late.
Molim Vas požurite. Kasnim.

Stop here!
Stanite ovdje!

How much is the ride from here to the hotel?
Koliko stoji vožnja odavde do hotela?

I want to get out here.
Želim izići ovdje.

Please wait a minute.
Molim Vas pričekajte minutu.

Wait until I come back.
Čekajte dok se vratim.

Wait for me here.
Čekajte me ovdje.

Drive a little farther.
Vozite malo dalje.

Please drive carefully.
Molim Vas, vozite pažljivo.

Be careful!
Oprezno!

Please drive slowly.
Molim Vas, vozite polako.

Watch out!
Pazite!

Turn left/right here.
Skrenite lijevo/desno ovdje.

Drive straight ahead.
Vozite ravno.

How much do I owe you?
Koliko Vam dugujem?

I need a taxi tomorrow.
Treba mi taksi sutra.

Please come to the hotel/here at eight o'clock.
Molim Vas dođite u hotel/ovamo u osam sati.

BUSES AND TRAMS (STREETCARS)

I would like to go by bus to...
Želim ići autobusom do...

Where is the bus station?
Gdje je autobusni kolodvor?

Where is the bus stop?
Gdje staje autobus?

Which bus/tram goes downtown?
Koji autobus/tramvaj vozi do centra grada?

Bus number 52.
Autobus broj 52.

Does the bus stop here?
Staje li autobus ovdje?

Does this tram go to Gajeva?
Ide li ovaj tramvaj do Gajeve?

Does this bus go to the airport?
Ide li ovaj autobus do uzletišta?

Tell me when we arrive at Klaić Street.
Recite mi kada dođemo do klaićeve ulice.

Where do I get on the streetcar?
Gdje uzimam tramvaj?

Get on the tram here.
Uzmite tramvaj ovdje.

Get off the bus here.
Siđite sa autobusa ovdje.

Does this bus go to the museum?
Ide li ovaj autobus do muzeja?

Do I need to change buses?
Trebam li presjedati?

You transfer to a bus that goes outside the city.
Presjedate na autobus koji ide van grada.

How long will it take?
Koliko će dugo uzeti?

What is the fare?
Koliko dođe vozna karta?

It takes one hour to get there.
Treba sat vremena da stignemo tamo.

Where must I transfer?
Gdje trebam presjedati?

Please tell me where to get off.
Molim Vas, recite mi gdje trebam sići.

When is the next bus?
Kada ide slijedeći autobus?

The next bus comes in fifteen minutes.
Slijedeći autobus dolazi za petnaest minuta.

How often do buses run?
Kako često idu autobusi?

They run every half hour.
Idu svaki pola sata.

When does the last bus leave?
Kada polazi zadnji autobus?

Please help me. I've taken the wrong bus.
Molim Vas pomozite mi. Uzeo/uzela sam krivi autobus

Please tell me which bus to take.
Molim Vas recite mi koji autobus da uzmem.

Take tram number 7.
Uzmite tramvaj broj sedam.

Please help me with my luggage.
Molim Vas pomozite mi sa prtljagom.

GETTING AROUND BY TRAIN

The railroad is a very frequently used means of transportation in Croatia. The trains are generally modern and comfortable. The priority and speed of the train is indicated by its category—local, intercity express or international express. Trains may be crowded in season, so it's a good idea to book seats and sleeping accomodations in advance.

The railroad station.
(Željeznički) kolodvor.

The train.
Vlak.

Drive to the railroad station.
Vozite do (željezničkog) kolodvora.

I need a porter.
Trebam portira.

Porter, this is my luggage.
Portiru, ovo je moja prtljaga.

These are my bags.
Ovo je moja prtljaga.

Here are the baggage checks.
Evo potvrda za prtljagu.

Where is the ticket window?
Gdje je šalter za karte?

DOLASCI ODLASCI

Have you a time-table?
Imate li vozni red?

When does the train leave?
Kada polazi vlak?

From which platform?
Sa kojeg perona?

I want to check this baggage.
Želim predati ovu prtljagu.

I must pick up a ticket.
Moram podignuti kartu.

I want two tickets to Rijeka on the four o'clock tomorrow.
Želim dvije karte za Rijeku u četiri sata sutra.

...a first class ticket.	*...a second class ticket.*
...prvorazrednu kartu.	**...drugorazrednu kartu.**
a one way ticket.	*...a round trip ticket.*
...jednosmjernu kartu.	**...povratnu kartu.**
...a sleeper.	*...a couchette.*
...spavaća kola.	**...kušet.**

Is there an earlier/later train?
Ima li vlak ranije/kasnije?

Is there a dining car on this train?
Ima li vagon-restoran na ovom vlaku?

Does this train go to....?
Ide li ovaj vlak do....?

Do I need to change?
Trebam li mijenjati?

Where do I change?
Gdje trebam mijenjati?

Is this the train for...?
Je li ovo vlak za...?

Does the train stop at?
Staje li vlak u...?

How long does it stop?
Koliko dugo stoji?

Is this train late?
Kasni li ovaj vlak?

It's ten minutes late.
Kasni deset minuta.

We have reserved seats.
Imamo rezervacije.

This is my seat.
Ovo je moje mjesto.

Is this seat occupied?
Je li ovo mjesto zauzeto?

This seat is taken.
Ovo je mjesto zauzeto.

Please sit down.
Molim Vas sjednite.

Where's the conductor?
Gdje je kondukter?

What is the next station?
Koja je iduća postaja?

What is the name of this station?
Kako se zove ova postaja?

How long do we stop here?
Koliko dugo stajemo ovdje?

Why has the train stopped?
Zašto je vlak stao?

There's been a breakdown.
Vlak je u kvaru.

May I smoke here?
Mogu li pušiti ovdje?

In the next car.
U drugim kolima.

May I open the window?
Mogu li otvoriti prozor?

Close the door.
Zatvorite vrata.

I have missed the train!
Promašio/promašila sam vlak!

When does the next train leave?
Kada polazi slijedeći vlak?

Where is the waiting room?
Gdje je čekaonica?

Where is the washroom?
Gdje je zahod?

The train is arriving now.
Vlak stiže sada.

All aboard!
Vlak kreće.

Tickets, please.
Karte, molim.

The train for Karlovac is leaving from platform five.
Vlak za Karlovac polazi sa perona broj pet.

The train from Zagreb is arriving on platform three.
Vlak iz Zagreba dolazi na peron broj tri.

Arrivals.
Dolasci.

Departures.
Odlasci.

Express train.
Brzi vlak.

Local train.
Lokalni vlak.

International express train.
Medjunarodni brzi vlak.

GETTING AROUND BY SHIP OR AIRPLANE

Going abroad by airplane may afford you the first opportunity to use Croatian. Although most attendants will speak some English, flight personnel will be especially attentive when you make an attempt to speak in Croatian. Travelling by ship can be a real adventure made much more exciting if you can make yourself understood by staff and by other passengers. The following phrases will help to make your travel especially rewarding.

SHIPS

Is there a boat/car ferry from here to Brač?
Ide li brod/trajekt odavde do Brača?

Where's the harbor (the port)?   *Where is the pier?*
Gdje je luka?   **Gdje je pristanište?**

What time does the ship sail?
U koliko sati polazi brod?

When will we board?
Kada ćemo se ukrcati?

How often do boats leave?
Kako često polaze brodovi?

How long does it take to get to Hvar?
Koliko dugo uzme da stignemo do Hvara?

I'd like to book a single berth cabin.
Želim rezervirati kabinu s jednim ležajem.

How many berths are there in this cabin?
Koliko ova kabina ima ležaja?

Where is cabin number 312?
Gdje je kabina broj 312?

Is this my cabin?
Je li ovo moja kabina?

Steward, do you have the key to my cabin?
Stjuard, imate li ključ od moje kabine?

I'm looking for the dining room.
Tražim blagovaonicu.

We want...
Želimo...

... a table for two.
...stol za dvoje.

..a. first-class cabin.
...prvorazrednu kabinu.

...a second-class cabin.
....drugorazrednu kabinu.

Let's go on deck.
Hajdemo na palubu.

I would like a deck chair.
Želim ležaljku.

I would like to eat by the swimming pool.
Želim jesti kraj bazena.

When do we dock?
Kada pristajemo?

When will we go ashore?
Kada ćemo se iskrcati?

The ship arrives at seven o'clock.
Brod stiže u sedam sati.

Where is the gangplank?
Gdje su vanjske stepenice?

How long do we stay in dock?
Koliko dugo ostajemo u luci?

Have a good trip!
Sretan Put!

AIRPLANES

Where is the Croatia Airlines office?
Gdje je ured od Croatia Airlines?

I want to go to the airport.
Želim ići na uzletište/do aerodroma.

Is there a bus that goes to the airport?
Ima li autobus koji ide na uzletište/do aerodroma?

I'd like to change my reservation.
Želim promijeniti rezervaciju.

Do you fly to Zadar?
Letite li u Zadar?

Is it a non-stop flight?
Je li to direktan let?

What is the fare?
Koliko dođe karta?

What's the flight number?
Koji je broj leta?

When does the plane leave?
Kada polazi zrakoplov?

When does it arrive?
Kada stiže?

Flight number 324 leaves at six o'clock.
Let broj 324 polazi u šest sati.

From which gate?
Sa kojeg izlaza?

I want to reconfirm my flight.
Želim potvrditi moj let.

When must I check in?
Kada se trebam prijaviti za let?

Ticket, please.
Kartu, molim.

Please fasten your seat belts.
Molim Vas zakopčajte Vaše sigurnosne pojase.

No smoking.
Zabranjeno pušenje.

Stewardess, give me a small pillow please.
Stjuardesa, molim Vas dajte mi mali jastuk.

I fly to Europe every year.
Letim u Europu svake godine.

The airplane is taking off.
Zrakoplov kreće.

Is a meal served during this flight?
Servira li se obrok za vrijeme ovoga leta?

The airplane will land in ten minutes.
Zrakoplov će sletiti za deset minuta.

There will be a delay.
Kasnit ćemo.

There's the runway.
Eno pista.

We have arrived!
Stigli smo!

SIGHTSEEING

Sightseeing will most likely be one of your major activities in Croatia. Because the country has over a thousand-year history with a rich cultural heritage, there is no shortage of attractions. Activities will be varied, therefore we could not possibly provide phrases for every situation. Use the words in the dictionary at the back of the book to supplement the phrases given here. If you join a tour, ask the guide to help you with your Croatian. Tour guides will be equally anxious to practice their English with you.

Where is the tourist office?
Gdje je turistički ured?

Can you recommend a good guide book about Zagreb?
Možete li preporučiti dobru knjigu, vodič o Zagrebu?

I would like to see the city.
Volio/voljela bih vidjeti grad.

Is there a sightseeing tour of...?
Ima li kakav izlet za turističko razgledavanje...?

How long does the tour last?
Koliko dugo traje tura?

We are going to see...
Idemo vidjeti...

It lasts three hours.
Traje tri sata.

Are you the guide?
Jeste li Vi vodič?

What is your name, please?
Molim Vas, kako se Vi zovete?

Do you speak English?
Govorite li engleski?

I speak only a few words of Croatian.
Ja govorim samo nekoliko riječi hrvatski.

What time does the tour start?
U koliko sati počinje tura?

We will leave the hotel at ten o'clock.
Polazimo iz hotela u deset sati.

What time will we return?
U koliko sati se vraćamo?

We'll return at three o'clock.
Vraćamo se u tri sata.

Can we eat there?
Možemo li jesti tamo?

Do we need tickets?
Trebamo li ulaznice?

No, it's free.
Ne, ne plaća se.

Have you a ticket?
Imate li ulaznicu?

Where do we buy tickets?
Gdje se kupe ulaznice?

How much are tickets?
Koliko su ulaznice?

Tickets are one dollar per person.
Ulaznice su dolar po osobi.

How are we going to get there?   *By bus.*
Kako ćemo doći tamo?   **Autobusom.**

What is the name of this place?   *It's called...*
Kako se zove ovo mjesto?   **Zove se...**

When was this place built?
Kada je ovo mjesto sagrađeno?

Five hundred years ago.   *It's beautiful.*
Prije petsto godina.   **Prekrasno je.**

May we go in?   *Yes, please do.*
Možemo li ući?   **Da, izvolite.**

May we take pictures?   *Please take our picture.*
Smije li se slikati?   **Molim Vas, slikajte nas.**

Can we buy a guidebook?
Možemo li kupiti džepni vodič?

Yes. It's not expensive.
Da. Nije skupo.

Are the museums closed on Sunday?
Jesu li muzeji zatvoreni nedjeljom?

The museums are open today.
Muzeji su otvoreni danas.

I wish to visit an art museum.
Želim posjetiti muzej umjetnosti.

Is there an exhibition there now?
Ima li izložba tamo sada?

What is the name of that church?
Kako se zove ta crkva?

This is the main square of the city.
Ovo je glavni trg grada.

We have walked a lot.
Puno smo hodali.

I am tired.
Ja sam umoran/umorna.

I need to rest for a few minutes.
Moram odmoriti nekoliko minuta.

Let's sit down a bit.
Hajdemo malo sjesti.

Where does this street lead?
Kuda vodi ova ulica?

To the cathedral.
Do katedrale.

What is that monument?
Što je onaj spomenik?

Is that a theater?
Je li to kazalište?

That's a movie house.
To je kino dvorana.

Where are the botanical gardens?
Gdje je botanički vrt?

We cross the street here.
Prelazimo ulicu ovdje.

What is the name of this river?
Kako se zove ova rijeka?

This is the longest bridge in the city.
Ovo je najduži most u gradu.

This is a large zoo.
Ovo je veliki zoološki vrt.

May we stay longer?
Možemo li ostati duže?

We must go back.
Moramo se vratiti.

We would like to come again.
Voljeli bismo doći ponovo.

SIGHTSEEING TERMS

academy	akademija	lake	jezero
aquarium	akvarij	library	knjižnica
archeology	arheologija	market	tržnica
architecture	arhitektura	medicine	medicina
art	umjetnost	memorial	spomen
art gallery	galerija umjetnosti	monastery	samostan
		monument	spomenik
artist	umjetnik	mosque	džamija
botanical garden	botanički vrt	mountain	gora
		music	glazba
bridge	most	observatory	zvjezdarnica
building	zgrada	old city	stari grad
business center	poslovni centar	opera house	operna dvorana
castle	dvorac/kaštel	painting	slikarstvo
cathedral	katedrala	palace	palača
cemetery	groblje	park	park
ceramics	keramika	parliament building	sabornica
city center	centar grada		
city hall	gradska vjećnica	peninsula	poluotok
church	crkva	planetarium	planetarij
coins	kovanice	pottery	keramika
concert hall	koncertna dvorana	river	rijeka
		ruins	ruševine
court house	sudnica	sculpture	kiparstvo
crafts	rukotvorine	seafront	dio grada uz obalu
dock	pristanište		
downtown area	centar grada	shopping center	trgovački centar
exhibition	ižložba		
factory	tvornica	shore	obala
fine arts	umjetnost	stadium	stadion
folk art	rukotvorine	statue	kip
fortress	tvrđava	stock exchange	burza
fountain	fontana/ vodoskok	synagogue	sinagoga
		theater	kazalište
furniture	namještaj	tomb	grob
garden(s)	vrt	tower	toranj
harbour	luka	university	sveučilište
history	povijest	village	selo
island	otok	zoo	zoološki vrt

RELIGIOUS SERVICES

Most Croatians are of the Roman Catholic faith. Churches are generally open during specific times. Hours of visitation are posted. There are also sizeable communities of other faiths, Eastern Orthodox, Protestant, Moslem and Jewish.

Is there a ... near here?
Ima li ... u blizini?

...Catholic church
...katolička crkva

....Protestant church
...protestantska crkva

...Orthodox church.
...pravoslavna crkva

...mosque
...džamija

...synagogue
...sinagoga

At what time is the mass/the service?
U koliko je sati misa/služba?

Does the priest speak english?
Govori li svećenik engleski?

RECREATION AND LEISURE

Croatia is a land of many contrasts and many forms of entertainment. With countless ways to relax, the coast has for centuries been the haven for aristocracy and simple folks alike. Seaside activities are fun for adults and children—swimming, collecting seashells and fascinating stones and constructing sand castles. Both summer and winter sports are very popular. The following phrases will help you to get the most out of your vacation.

AT THE BEACH, SAILING & FISHING

Where are the best beaches?
Gdje su najbolje plaže?

Is there a quiet beach around here?
Ima li mirna plaža u blizini?

Can we walk?
Možemo li ići pješke?

Is there a bus to the beach?
Ide li autobus do plaže?

Is the sea rough around here?
Je li ovdje more nemirno?

The sea is very calm.
More je vrlo mirno.

There are some big waves.
Ima velikih valova.

Is it safe for swimming?
Je li sigurno za plivanje?

Is it a good beach for children?
Je li to dobra plaža za djecu?

Bathing/swimming prohibited.
Zabranjeno kupanje.

Diving prohibited.
Zabranjeno skakanje u vodu.

Is it a good place for snorkeling?
Je li to dobro mjesto za ronjenje?

What is the temperature of the water?
Kolika je temperatura vode?

We would like to go fishing.
Želimo ići u ribolov.

I want to buy/rent ...	*...a bath towel.*
Hoću kupiti/iznajmiti...	**...kupaći ručnik.**
...a bathing suit.	*...a deck chair.*
...kupaći kostim.	**...ležaljku.**
...skin diving equipment.	*...suntan lotion.*
...ronilačku opremu.	**...losion za sunčanje.**
...water skis.	*...a boat/a canoe.*
...skije na vodi.	**...čamac/kanu.**
...a motor boat.	*...a sailboat.*
...motorni čamac.	**...jedrilicu.**
....fish-hooks.	*...a fishing rod.*
...udice.	**...štap za ribanje.**
...fishing tackle.	
...pribor za ribanje.	

CAMPING AND HIKING

Is there a footpath to...
Ima li pješačka staza do...

Is there a short-cut?
Ima li preki put?

Is there drinking water available?
Ima li pitke vode?

Is there a camping site near here?
Ima li kampiralište u blizini?

May we camp here?
Smijemo li kampirati ovdje?

May we light a fire?
Smijemo li ložiti vatru?

Does the campground have showers and toilets?
Ima li kampiralište tuševe i zahode?

May we park here?
Možemo li parkirati ovdje?

Where can I buy butane gas/kerosene?
Gdje mogu kupiti plin/petrolej?

Can we rent a tent?
Možemo li iznajmiti šator?

Where can I dispose of the garbage?
Gdje mogu baciti smeće?

SPORTS AND GAMES

I would like to go to a soccer game.
Ja bih volio/voljela ići na nogometnu utakmicu.

Who's playing?
Tko igra?

Where is the stadium/the race course?
Gdje je stadion/trkalište?

Please give me three tickets.
Molim Vas dajte mi tri ulaznice.

Do you have any cheaper tickets?
Imate li jeftinijih ulaznica?

When does it start?
Kada počinje?

When does it end?
Kada završava?

Who is winning?
Tko pobjeđuje?

Where can I/we...
Gdje mogu/možemo...

...play tennis?
...igrati tenis?

...go skiing?
...ići na skijanje?

...go skating?
...ići na klizanje?

...go bowling?
...ići na kuglanje?

...go horse-back riding?
...ići na jahanje?

Where is there a swimming pool?
Gdje ima kupaći bazen?

Is it indoor or outdoor?
Je li pod krovom ili vani?

Is it heated?
Je li grijan?

Where are the thermal springs?
Gdje su toplice?

Where is there a good sports shop?
Gdje ima dobra trgovina športske opreme?

What is the charge per hour?
Koliko se naplaćuje po satu?

I would like to rent...	*...skis*	*...skates*
Želim iznajmiti...	**...skije**	**...klizaljke**
	...a boat	*...a bicycle*
	...čamac	**...kotur/bicikl**

GOING OUT ON THE TOWN

During the tourist season Croatia's coastal towns and major cities live twenty-four hours a day. There are numerous theaters and concert halls, discos, nightclubs and even gambling casinos. The luxury hotel that caters to business people and museum lovers during the day may run a lively night club with a floor show and dancing at night. Ask the local travel agency about the floating dance halls that cruise the Adriatic nightly, stopping at fishing villages for more singing and dancing. Concerts may feature rock music, folk music and dancing or even classical music in magnificent settings.

Where shall we go tonight?
Kuda ćemo izići večeras?

Let's go ...	*...to see the ballet.*
Hajdemo ...	**...gledati balet.**

...to a concert.
...na koncert.

...to the opera.
...slušati operu.

...to the theater.
...u kazalište.

...to see a movie.
...u kino.

...to see a foreign film.
...gledati strani film.

...to a bar/nightclub.
...u bar/noćni klub.

...to a disco.
...u disko.

...to a casino.
...u kasino.

...to see folk dancing.
...na folklor.

....dancing.
...na ples.

...to the circus.
...u cirkus.

Can we find someone to take care of the children?
Možemo li naći nekoga da čuva djecu?

How should I dress?
Kako se trebam obući?

You can wear anything you like.
Možete obući što god želite.

Black tie.   *Casual dress.*   *Evening wear.*
Svečano.   **Sportska odjeća.**   **Večernja odjeća.**

What time does it start?
U koliko sati počinje?

Is food served there?
Hoće li se hrana servirati tamo?

Can we buy drinks?
Može li se kupiti piće?

What time does it end?
U koliko sati završava?

Do we need tickets?
Trebamo li ulaznice?

Can we get tickets at the door?
Mogu li se kupiti ulaznice tamo?

Where do we buy tickets?
Gdje se kupe ulaznice?

Please help me buy tickets for...
Molim Vas pomozite mi kupiti ulaznice za...

INVITATIONS

I would like to invite you to dinner.
Želim Vas pozvati na večeru.

I'm very happy to accept. Thank you.
Drago mi je prihvatiti poziv. Hvala.

What time shall we go?
U koliko sati ćemo ići?

Where shall we meet?
Gdje ćemo se sastati?

In front of the hotel.
Ispred hotela.

Under the clock at Jelačić Square.
Ispod sata na Jelačićevom trgu.

May I bring a friend?
Mogu li povesti prijatelja/prijateljicu?

Of course [you may].
Sigurno [da možete].

Where shall we eat?
Gdje ćemo jesti?

Let's eat at the Dubrovnik Restaurant.
Jedimo u restoranu Dubrovnik.

MAKING FRIENDS

How do you do?/How are you?
Kako ste?

My name is...
Ja se zovem...

May I introduce...
Dopustite da Vam predstavim...

How long have you been in Croatia?
Koliko ste dugo u Hrvatskoj?

I've been here ten days.
Ovdje sam deset dana.

I am from Britain/Canada/the United States.
Ja sam iz Velike Britanije/Kanade/Amerike.

I speak English/French/German /Italian/Spanish.
**Govorim engleski/francuski/njemački/talijanski/
španjolski.**

Are you enjoying yourself?
Zabavljate li se dobro?

We're having a wonderful time.
Divno se zabavljamo.

Did you come alone?
Jeste li došli sami?

No, I came with my husband.
Ne, došla sam sa mojim suprugom.

No, I came with my wife.
Ne, došao sam sa mojom suprugom.

...with my family.
... s mojom obitelji.

...with my friends.
...s mojim prijateljima.

...with my friend. (masc.)
...s mojim prijateljem.

...with my friend. (fem.)
...s mojom prijateljicom.

What places have you visited?
Koja ste mjesta posjetili?

I've been to Zagreb.
Bio/bila sam u Zagrebu.

... to the coast.
...na moru.

Where else are you going?
Kamo još idete?

We'll be going to...	*Have you been to...?*
Ići ćemo u...	**Jeste li bili u...?**

Yes, I have.	*No, I haven't.*
Da, jesam.	**Ne, nisam.**

What brings you to Croatia?
Što Vas je donijelo u Hrvatsku?

I am here on vacation.
Ja sam tu na odmoru.

I am...
Ja sam...

...a businessman	*...a housewife*	*...a writer*
...poslovni čovjek	**...domačica**	**...pisac**
...a doctor	*...a scientist*	*...a singer*
...liječnik	**...naučnik**	**...pjevač**
...a dentist	*...a teacher*	*...a secretary*
...stomatolog	**...učitelj(ica)**	**...tajnik/tajnica**
...an attorney	*...an artist*	
...odvjetnik	**...umjetnik**	

I am a student.
Ja sam student(ica).

I'm studying medicine.
Studiram medicinu.

Where do you go to school?
Gdje studirate?

I attend Zagreb University.
Studiram na zagrebačkom sveučilištu.

I'm travelling on business.
Putujem poslovno.

Would you like a cigarette?
Izvolite cigaretu.

Do you have a light, please?
Imate li vatre, molim Vas?

Can I buy you a drink?
Mogu li Vas počastiti pićem?

Are you waiting for someone?
Čekate li nekoga?

Are you free this evening?
Jeste li slobodni večeras?

Would you like to go out with me tonight?
Želite li izići sa mnom večeras?

Would you like to go dancing this evening?
Želite li ići na ples večeras?

I'd love to.
Bit će mi drago.

Let's go for a drive.
Hajdemo se provesti.

May I take you home?
Mogu li Vas odvesti doma?

Where are you staying?
Gdje odsjedate?

Where do you live?
Gdje stanujete?

May I have your address?
Mogu li imati Vašu adresu?

Can I see you again tomorrow?
Možemo li se vidjeti opet sutra?

What's your telephone number?
Koji je Vaš broj telefona?

Thank you. It's been a wonderful evening.
Hvala. Bilo je prekrasno.

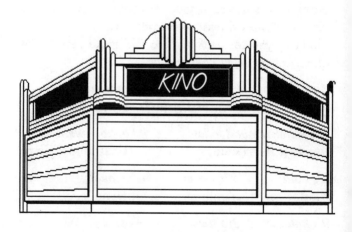

WEATHER

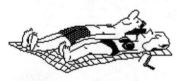

Weather is a universal topic of conversation. You can easily learn the expressions provided in this section. They will help you to break the ice and make new friends wherever you might be travelling.

How is the weather?	*It's nice weather today.*
Kako je vrijeme?	**Lijepo je vrijeme danas.**

The weather's bad today.	*What horrible weather!*
Danas je nevrijeme.	**Užasno je vrijeme!**

It's cold.	*It's warm.*	*It's cloudy.*
Hladno je.	**Toplo je.**	**Oblačno je.**

It's hot.	*It's humid.*	*It's sunny.*
Vruće je.	**Sparno je.**	**Sunčano je.**

Is it raining?
Pada li kiša?

It has stopped raining.
Kiša je prestala.

Yes, it's raining.
Da, pada kiša.

Look, the sun has come out.
Pogledajte, sunce je izišlo.

No, it's not raining.
Ne, ne pada kiša.

It's windy.
Vjetrovito je.

It's snowing.
Pada snijeg.

It's foggy today.
Maglovito je danas.

It's really pretty.
Prekrasno je.

The sun is rising.
Izlazi sunce.

It never snows here.
Tu nikada ne pada snijeg.

The sun is setting.
Zalazi sunce.

It rains there every day.
Tamo svaki dan pada kiša.

Will it be cool there?
Hoće li biti svježe tamo?

It's beginning to rain.
Kiša počinje.

Will it be damp there?
Hoće li biti vlažno tamo?

I need an umbrella
Treba mi kišobran.

Do I need...
Trebam li...

It often rains here.
Ovdje često pada kiša.

... a raincoat?
...kabanicu?

It will rain tomorrow.
Padat će kiša sutra.

...a jacket?
...jaknu?

It rained yesterday.
Jučer je kiša padala.

...a sweater?
...džemper?

It's lightning.
Baca se munja.

It's thundering.
Grmi.

WEATHER VOCABULARY

cold weather	**hladno vrijeme**	*the sky*	**nebo**
warm weather	**toplo vrijeme**	*the sun*	**sunce**
nice weather	**ugodno vrijeme**	*the moon*	**mjesec**
bad weather	**nevrijeme**	*the stars*	**zvijezde**
sunny	**sunčano**	*a star*	**zvijezda**
cloudy	**oblačno**	*a rainbow*	**duga**
the rain	**kiša**	*a cloud*	**oblak**
the wind	**vjetar**	*clouds*	**oblaci**
snow	**snijeg**	*lightning*	**munja**
ice	**led**	*thunder*	**grom**
		a storm	**oluja**

NUMBERS, TIME AND DATES

You will need to know the essentials of counting and telling time to count your change, make an appointment or to catch a plane. Like the rest of Europe, Croatia uses a twenty-four hour system for schedules and timetables. Thus 8:00 PM in Croatia would be expressed as 20:00 hours and 9:30 PM is 21:30.

CARDINAL NUMBERS

0	ništica	14	četernaest	28	dvadeset osam
1	jedan	15	petnaest	29	dvadeset devet
2	dva	16	šestnaest	30	trideset
3	tri	17	sedamnaest	31	trideset jedan
4	četiri	18	osamnaest	32	trideset dva
5	pet	19	devetnaest	40	četrdeset
6	šest	20	dvadeset	50	pedeset
7	sedam	21	dvadeset jedan	51	pedeset jedan
8	osam	22	dvadeset dva	52	pedeset dva
9	devet	23	dvadeset tri	56	pedeset šest
10	deset	24	dvadeset četiri	60	šezdeset
11	jedanaest	25	dvadest pet	70	sedamdeset
12	dvanaest	26	dvadeset šest	80	osamdeset
13	trinaest	27	dvadeset sedam	90	devedeset

100	sto	*one thousand*	tisuća
200	dvjesto	*one million*	milijun
300	tristo	*one day*	jedan dan
400	četiristo	*two days*	dva dana
500	petsto	*many days*	mnogo dana
600	šeststo	*one ticket*	jedna ulaznica
700	sedamsto	*two tickets*	dvije ulaznice
800	osamsto	*one seat*	jedno sjedište
900	devetsto	*two seats*	dva sjedišta

ORDINAL NUMBERS

the first	prvi	*the tenth*	deseti
the second	drugi	*the first man*	prvi čovjek
the third	treći	*the first woman*	prva žena
the fourth	četvrti	*the first child*	prvo dijete
the fifth	peti	*the second*	druga
the sixth	šesti	*building*	zgrada
the seventh	sedmi	*the third day*	treći dan
the eighth	osmi	*the fourth street*	četvrta ulica
the ninth	deveti	*the fifth floor*	peti kat

TELLING TIME

What time is it?
Koliko je sati?

Excuse me, can you tell me what time it is?
Oprostite, možete li mi reći koliko je sati?

My watch has stopped.
Stao mi je sat.

It's one o'clock.
Jedan je sat.

It's two o'clock.
Dva sata je.

It's ten to two.
Deset je do dva.

It's a quarter after three.
Tri i petnaest je.

It's ten after five.
Pet i deset je.

It's a quarter to seven now.
Sada je petanest do sedam.
Sada je tri četvrt sedam.

It's eleven o'clock.
Jedanaest je sati.

It's ten o'clock.
Deset je sati.

It's noon.	**Podne je.**
It's midnight.	**Ponoć je.**
It's early.	**Rano je.**
It's late.	**Kasno je.**
after	**poslije**
before	**prije**
on time	**na vrijeme**
one second	**jedna sekunda**
five seconds	**pet sekundi**
one minute	**jedna minuta**
five minutes	**pet minuta**
fifteen minutes	**petnaest minuta**
one quarter hour	**(jedan) četvrt sata**
one half hour	**pol(a) sata**
one hour	**jedan sat**
five hours	**pet sati**

At what time are you leaving?
U koliko sati polazite?

Be here at five o'clock.
Budite tu u pet sati.

What time do you arrive?
U koliko sati stižete?

At what time do you get up?
U koliko sati ustajete?

What time will we arrive?
U koliko sati stižemo?

What time do you go to bed?
U koliko sati legnete?

When shall we meet?
Kada ćemo se sastati?

DATES

today	danas	last month	prošli mjesec
tomorrow	sutra	last year	prošle godine
yesterday	jučer	this week	ovaj tjedan
one day	jedan dan	this month	ovaj mjesec
two days	dva dana	this year	ove godine
five days	pet dana	next week	idući tjedan
the day after		next month	idući mjesec
tomorrow	preksutra	next year	iduća godina
the day before		this morning	jutros
yesterday	prekjučer	yesterday	jučer ujutro
the morning	jutro	morning	
in the morning	ujutro	tomorrow	sutra ujutro
the afternoon	poslije podne	morning	
the evening	večer	this evening	večeras
in the evening	uvečer	yesterday	sinoć
the night	noć	evening	
at night	po noći	last night	prošle noći
the week	tjedan	tomorrow	
the month	mjesec	evening	sutra navečer
the year	godina	every day	svaki dan
last week	prošli tjedan	two days ago	prije dva dana

DAYS OF THE WEEK

Monday	ponedjeljak	Sunday	nedjelja
Tuesday	utorak	Wednesday	u srijedu
Wednesday	srijeda	evening	navečer
Thursday	četvrtak	Sunday	u nedjelju
Friday	petak	morning	ujutro
Saturday	subota	every Tuesday	svaki utorak

MONTHS OF THE YEAR

January	siječanj	July	srpanj
February	veljača	August	kolovoz
March	ožujak	September	rujan
April	travanj	October	listopad
May	svibanj	November	studeni
June	lipanj	December	prosinac

since May
od svibnja

during the month of December
u prosincu

October 1	*3/13/1995*
1 listopada	**13.3.1995.**
What's the date?	*It's December 3.*
Koji je datum?	**Treći je prosinca.**

We've leaving on July 17.
Odlazimo 17og srpnja.

We arrived in Croatia on April 12.
Stigli smo u Hrvatsku 12og travnja.

Like other European countries, Croatia writes the day before the month when writing out a date. Thus 10.08.1994. would be the tenth of August 1994 which in English would normally be written 08/10/94.

THE SEASONS

the spring	**proljeće**	*next fall*	**na jesen**
the summer	**ljeto**	*during the winter*	**preko zime**
the autumn	**jesen**	*in the spring*	**u proljeće**
the winter	**zima**	*last summer*	**prošlog ljeta**

SPECIAL DAYS AND HOLIDAYS

holiday	*workday/weekday*	*non workday*
blagdan	**radni dan**	**praznik**
vacation	*school holidays*	*weekend*
odmor	**školski praznici**	**vikend**

All Saints' Day. (November 1)
Blagdan svih svetih.

Anniversary   *Happy anniversary!*
Godišnjica   **Sretna godišnjica!**

Bairam
Bajram

Birthday
Rođendan

birthday gift
poklon za rođendan

Happy Birthday!
Sretan Rođendan!

Christmas.
Božić.

Christmas holidays.
Božićni blagdani.

Christmas Eve.   *Merry Christmas.*
Badnjak.   **Sretan Božić.**

Graduation   *Congratulations!*
Diplomiranje   **Čestitam.**

Easter.
Uskrs.

Easter holidays.
Uskrsni blagdani.

Happy Easter!
Sretan Uskrs!

Mother's Day.
Majčin dan.

Happy Mother's Day
Sretan Majčin Dan!

New Year's Day.
Nova Godina.

New Year's Eve.
Silvestrovo.

Happy New Year!
Sretna Nova Godina!

Father's Day.
Očev dan.

Happy Father's Day!
Sretan Očev Dan!

Hanukkah.
Hanuka.

Happy Hanukkah!
Sretna Hanuka!

Independence Day. (May 30)
Trideseti svibnja.

Labor Day. (May 1)
Prvi svibanj.

Valentine's Day.
Sveti Valentin.

Happy Valentine's Day.
Sretan Sveti Valentin.

Wedding Anniversary.
Svadbeni pir.

HEALTH AND MEDICAL

Much as we hope that one will never need the phrases provided in this section, one does get sick when travelling. The doctor's diagnosis may well depend on what you, the patient tell him is wrong with you, so you will want to make yourself clearly understood. If you have any serious health problem, it would be a good idea to carry a copy of your prescription with you and always carry a prescription for your glasses or contact lenses.

AT THE DOCTOR'S

I need a doctor.
Treba mi liječnik.

Send for a doctor.
Zovite liječnika.

I don't feel good.
Ja se ne osjećam dobro.

I am ill.
Bolestan/Bolesna sam.

Is there a doctor in the hotel?
Ima li liječnika u hotelu?

Please send the doctor to my room.
Molim Vas pošaljite liječnika u moju sobu.

My room number is...
Broj moje sobe je...

Where is the hospital?
Gdje je bolnica?

Is there a drugstore near here?
Ima li ljekarna u blizini?

Are you the doctor?
Jeste li Vi liječnik?

Do you speak English?
Govorite li engleski?

THE DIAGNOSIS

What is the matter with you?
Što Vam je?

Where does it hurt?
Gdje Vas boli?

It hurts here. (pointing)
Boli me tu.

Open your mouth.
Otvorite usta.

Lie down.
Legnite.

You may get up.
Možete ustati.

Stick out your tongue.
Isplazite jezik.

Do you smoke?	*Yes, I smoke.*
Pušite li?	**Da, pušim.**

No, I don't smoke.
Ne, ne pušim.

Do you sleep well?	*I sleep well.*
Spavate li dobro?	**Spavam dobro.**

I don't sleep well.
Ne spavam dobro.

How old are you?	*I'm 33 years old.*
Koliko imate godina?	**Imam 33 godina.**

Are you taking any medication now?
Uzimate li kakve lijekove?

Yes, I'm taking this medicine.
Da, uzimam ovaj lijek.

No, I'm not taking any medicine.
Ne, ne uzimam nikakve lijekove.

Do you have a good appetite?
Imate li dobar apetit?

I didn't eat yesterday.
Nisam jeo/jela jučer.

I have no appetite.
Nemam apetita.

I am a diabetic.
Ja sam dijabetičar.

I have a cardiac condition.
Ja sam srčani bolesnik.

I had a heart attack two years ago.
Imao/imala sam srčani napad prije dvije godine.

I am allergic to...
Ja sam alergičan na...

How long have you been sick?
Koliko ste dugo bolesni?

I have been ill for two days.
Ja sam bolestan/bolesna već dva dana.

I have a cold.
Prehlađen/prehlađena sam.

I have been vomiting.
Povraćao/povraćala sam.

I'm expecting a baby.
Ja sam u drugom stanju.

I have a headache.	*I have a stomachache.*
Boli me glava.	**Boli me želudac.**
I have a migraine.	*I have a backache.*
Imam migrenu.	**Bole me krsta.**

I have a cough.
Kašljem.

I have a sore throat.
Boli me grlo.

I have a runny nose.
Curi mi na nos.

My finger is bleeding.
Moj prst krvari.

I have a fever.
Imam groznicu.

I have burned myself.
Opekao/opekla sam se.

I can't move my...
Ne mogu micati...

My... is swollen.
Otekao/otekla mi je...

My... hurts.
Boli me...

PARTS OF THE BODY

ankle	**članak**	*heel*	**peta**
appendix	**slijepo crijevo**	*hip*	**kuk**
arm	**ruka**	*intestines*	**crijeva**
back	**krsta**	*jaw*	**vilica**
bladder	**mjehur**	*joint*	**zglob**
blood	**krv**	*kidney*	**bubreg**
bone	**kost**	*knee*	**koljeno**
chest	**grudi**	*leg*	**noga**
chin	**brada**	*lip*	**usna**
collar-bone	**ključna kost**	*liver*	**jetra**
ear	**uho**	*lungs*	**pluća**
elbow	**lakat**	*mouth*	**usta**
eye	**oko**	*muscles*	**mišići**
face	**lice**	*neck*	**vrat**
finger	**prst**	*nerve*	**živac**
foot	**noga**	*nose*	**nos**
gland	**žlijezda**	*rib*	**rebro**
hair	**kosa**	*shoulder*	**rame**
hand	**ruka**	*sinus*	**sinus**
head	**glava**	*skin*	**koža**
heart	**srce**	*spine*	**kičma**

stomach	želudac	tongue	jezik
thigh	bedro	tonsils	krajnici
throat	grlo	urine	mokraća
thumb	palac	vein	vena
toe	nožni prst	wrist	ručni zglob

AILMENTS

abscess	apsces	foodpoisoning	otrovanje želuca
arthritis	artritis	flu	gripa
asthma	astma	hay fever	peludna groznica
bee sting	ubod od pčele	high blood	visoki tlak
boil	čir	pressure	krvi
blister	žulj	indigestion	loša probava
broken	slomljen	influenza	gripa
bruise	modrica	insect bite	ubod od kukca
cold	prehlada	rheumatism	reuma
constipation	konstipacija	sunburn	opeklina od
cramps	grčevi u želucu		sunca
(stomach)		ulcer	čir na želucu
diarrhea	proljev	whooping	hripavac
fever	groznica	cough	

TREATMENT

You must stay in bed.
Morate ležati.

How long?
Koliko dugo?

At least two days.
Najmanje dva dana.

You should eat only bland food.
Trebate jesti samo blagu hranu.

Have you ever had ill effects from penicillin?
Jeste li ikada imali reakciju od penicilina?

I would like to have an x-ray made.
Volio bih ići na rendgen.

Have you been vaccinated against tetanus?
Jeste li dobili injekciju protiv tetanusa?

I will give you an injection.
Dat ću Vam injekciju.

It is/is not infected.
Zaraženo je/nije zaraženo.

You are seriously ill.
Vi ste vrlo bolesni.

Do I need to go to the hospital?
Trebam li ići u bolnicu?

No, that will not be necessary.
Ne, to neće biti potrebno.

Can I travel?
Mogu li putovati?

Don't worry. You'll feel better soon.
Nemojte brinuti. Uskoro ćete se bolje osjećati.

Take this medicine three times a day.
Uzimajte ovaj lijek tri puta na dan.

Here is a prescription.
Evo Vam recept.

How much each time?   *One teaspoonful.*
Koliko svaki puta?   **Jednu žličicu.**

I feel better now.   *Come again tomorrow.*
Osjećam se bolje sada.   **Đođite opet sutra.**

I will come later.
Doći ću kasnije.

He's a good doctor.
On je dobar liječnik.

AT THE DENTIST'S

Can you recommend a good dentist?
Možete li preporučiti dobrog stomatologa?

Can I see Dr. ... immediately?
Mogu li hitno vidjeti Dr....?

I've got a toothache.
Boli me zub.

I have an abscess.
Imam apsces.

This tooth hurts.
Ovaj me zub boli.

Can you fix it temporarily?
Možete li popraviti privremeno?

My gums are swollen.
Zubne desni su mi natekle.

My gums are bleeding.
Krvare mi zubne desni.

My tooth is loose.
Klima mi se zub.

Don't remove the tooth.
Nemojte izvaditi zub.

My tooth is broken.
Slomio mi se zub.

The filling has fallen out.
Ispala je blomba.

Can you fill it now?
Možete li blombirati sada?

Please give me an injection first.
Molim Vas dajte mi najprije injekciju.

I will x-ray your teeth.
Napravit ću rendgen od Vaših zubi.

You're hurting me.
Vrijeđate me.

When should I come again?
Kada da dođem ponovo?

I've broken my dentures.
Zubalo mi se slomilo.

Can you repair it?	*When will it be ready?*
Možete li popraviti?	**Kada će biti gotovo?**

AT THE OPTICIAN'S

Where is the nearest optician?
Gjde je najbliži optičar?

I've broken my glasses.
Razbio sam naočale.

Can you repair them?
Možete li ih povpraviti?

Can you change the lenses?
Možete li promijeniti stakla?

I've lost one of my contact lenses.
Izgubio/izgubila sam kontaktnu leću.

Can you replace it? Here is the prescription.
Možete li nabaviti drugu? Evo recept.

I'd like to buy sunglasses.
Želim kupiti sunčane naočale.

EMERGENCY SITUATIONS

We hope that you will never need to use any of the cries, commands or expressions that are provided in this section. Unfortunately, accidents do happen, items may be lost or stolen and mistakes do occur. Should an emergency arise, you will find the phrases below to help you. Just to be on the safe side, memorize those expressions that are shown in capital letters.

Call the police.
Zovite policiju.

Come here!
Dođi(te) ovamo!

CAREFUL!
OPREZNO!

Come in.
Uđite.

DANGER.
OPASNOST.

FIRE.
POŽAR.

Get a doctor.
Zovite liječnika.

Go away!
Idite!

HELP!
U POMOĆ!

I'm ill.
Bolestan/bolesna sam.

I'm lost.
Ja sam izgubljen(a).

Don't move.
Ne mići se.

Leave me alone.
Ostavite me na miru.

Listen.
Slušaj.

LOOK.
VIDI.

LOOK OUT.
PAZITE.

Police.
**Redarstvo/
Policija.**

Poison.
Otrov.

Quick.
Brzo.

STOP.
STANITE.

Stop here.
Stanite ovdje.

Thief.
Lopov.

Stop that man!
Zaustavite tog čovjeka!

Please help me.
Molim Vas pomozite mi.

Please help me get to the hotel.
Molim Vas pomozite mi doći do hotela.

Come with me.
Dođite sa mnom.

Where is the police station?
Gdje je redarstvena (policijska) ispostava?

Where is the American/Canadian embassy?
Gdje je američka/kanadska ambasada?

Please let the ambassador know.
Molim Vas javite ambasadoru.

My wallet/purse/passport has been stolen.
Ukrali su mi novčarku/torbu/putovnicu.

There has been an accident.
Dogodila se nesreća.

He's badly hurt.
Ozbiljno je povrijeđen.

She has fainted.
Pala je u nesvijest.

He's/she's losing blood.
Gubi krv.

Bring some water/a blanket/bandages.
Donesite vodu/deku/zavoje.

I have lost my...
Izgubio/izgubila sam...

my bags	**moje torbe**	*my traveller's*	**moje putničke**
my handbag	**moju torbu**	*checks*	**čekove**
my luggage	**moju prtljagu**	*my passport*	**moju**
my money	**moj novac**		**putovnicu**

Please give me a copy of the police report.
Molim Vas dajte mi kopiju redarstvenog izvještaja.

Thank you very much for your help.
Najljepša Vam hvala za pomoć.

Signs and Symbols

Even if you do not speak any Croatian, you should be able to get along if you can read signs and notices that are posted and displayed. Pronunciation is not important. Some of the following signs and symbols may help you avoid danger. Others might avoid embarrassment. Hopefully, they will all make life a little more pleasant.

AERODROM, *Airport*

AUTOBUSNI KOLODVOR, *Bus Station*

AUTOBUSNO STAJALIŠTE, *Bus Stop*

BLAGAJNA, *Cashier*

BLAGOVAONA, *Dining Room*

BOLNICA, *Hospital*

CARINA, *Customs*

CRKVA, *Church*

ČEKAONICA, *Waiting Room*

DOLAZAK, *Arrival*

GARDEROBA,*Cloakroom, Left Baggage*

GURNI, *Push*

HAK (Hrvatski Auto-Moto Klub),
   Croatian Automobile Association

HLADNO, *Cold*

HOTEL, *Hotel*

KATEDRALA, *Cathedral*

KAVANA, *Coffee Shop*

KUPAONA, *Bathroom*

INFORMACIJE, *Information*

IZLAZ, *Exit*

KAMPIRALIŠTE, *Campgrounds*

KAMPIRANJE, *Camping*

LIFT, *Elevator*

LUKA, *Port*

MJENJAČNICA, *Foreign Exchange Bureau*

MUŠKI, *Men's*

NE DIRATI, *Don't touch*

NEPITKA VODA, *Don't Drink the Water*

ODLAZAK, *Departure*

OPASNI ZAVOJ, *Dangerous Curve*

OPASNOST, *Danger*

OPREZ, *Warning*

OTVORENO, *Open*

OTVORENO OD... DO..., *Open from... to...*

PARKIRALIŠTE, *Parking*
PERON BROJ, *Platform no. (train station)*
PITKA VODA, *Drinking Water*
PJEŠACI, *Pedestrians*
POKRETNI MOST, *Drawbridge*
POLICIJA, *Police*
POLICIJSKA ISPOSTAVA, *Police Station*
POVUCI, *Pull*
POZOR, *Caution*
POZVONI, *Ring* (doorbell)
PREDAJA PRTLJAGE, *Baggage check*
PRODAJE SE, *For Sale*
PRVA POMOĆ, *First Aid*
RASPRODANO, *Sold out*
REDARSTVO, *Police*
REDARSTVENA ISPOSTAVA, *Police Station*
RESTORAN, *Restaurant*
REZERVIRANO, *Reserved*
SAMOPOSLUŽIVANJE, *Self-service*
SLASTIČARNA, *Pastry Shop*
SLIJEPA CESTA, *Dead End Street*
SNEK BAR, *Snack Bar*
SLOBODNO, *Vacant/free/unoccupied*
SNIŽENJE, *On sale*
SOBE ZA IZNAJMITI, *Rooms to Let*
SUŽENJE CESTE, *Road Narrows*

ŠKOLA, *School*
TAXI, *Taksi*
TELEFON, *Telephone*
TRAMVAJSKO STAJALIŠTE, *Tram Stop*
ULAZ, *Entrance*
ULAZ BESPLATAN, *Free Admission*
USKA CESTA, *Narrow Road*
USKI MOST, *Narrow Bridge*
UZLETIŠTE, *Airport*
VATROGASNA SLUŽBA, *Fire Station*
VRUĆE, *Hot*
ZABRANJEN PROMET, *No traffic*
ZABRANJEN ULAZ, *Keep Out*
ZABRANJENO, *Forbidden*
ZABRANJENO PARKIRANJE, *No Parking*
ZABRANJENO PUŠENJE, *No Smoking*
ZABRANJENO SKRETANJE UDESNO,
   No Right Turn
ZABRANJENO SKRETANJE ULIJEVO,
   No Left Turn
ZAHODI, *Toilets*
ZATVORENO, *Closed*
ZAUZETO, *Occupied*
ZAVOJ, *Curve*
ŽELJEZNIČKI KOLODVOR, *Railroad station*
ŽELJEZNIČKI PRIJELAZ, *Railway Crossing*
ŽENSKI, *Women's*

Some International Road Signs

No Vehicles

No Entry

Caution

No Parking

Max. Speed Limit

Intersection

Dangerous Curve

Road Narrows

Two-way Traffic

Dangerous Hill

Yield

Uneven Road

Falling Rocks

Main Road

End of Restriction

One-way Traffic

Minimum Speed Limit

Parking

Hospital

Highway

Filling Station

*Not a Through
Road*

*Pedestrians
Only*

No Left Turn

No Right Turn

No U turn

Slippery Road

Customs

No Parking

*No Stopping or
Parking*

*Direction to be
Followed*

No Passing

Right Curve

Double Curve

*Traffic
Circle*

Information

TIPS ON CROATIAN GRAMMAR

The grammatical structure of the Croatian language is quite complex. For that reason no attempt can be made to give more than a very brief outline of certain aspects of Croatian grammar. However, the following points will go a long way in helping you to put together simple sentences and to understand how the phrases in this book are constructed. By substituting one or two words in the sample sentences in this book, you will greatly increase your ability to understand and speak everyday Croatian.

Nouns and Gender

All Croatian nouns are divided into three genders: masculine, feminine and neuter. Feminine nouns generally end in the vowel **a.** They form the plural by changing the **a** to **e.**

Singular	Plural	
knjiga	**knjige**	*book(s)*
žena	**žene**	*woman/women*

Some feminine nouns (ususally abstract) end in a consonant. They form the plural by adding the ending **-i**

noć	**noći**	*night(s)*
riječ	**riječi**	*word(s)*

Neuter nouns generally end in the vowels **-o** or **-e**. They form the plural by changing the **-o** or **-e** to **-a.**

pismo	**pisma**	*letter(s)*
more	**mora**	*sea(s)*

Many neuter nouns insert a **-t** or an **-n** between the stem and the ending when forming the plural.

ime	**imena**	*name(s)*
dugme	**dugmeta**	*button(s)*

Masculine nouns generally end in a consonant. They form the plural by adding the vowel **-i** to the end of the word.

prozor	**prozori**	*window(s)*
tramvaj	**tramvaji**	*streetcar(s)*

Masculine nouns that are only one syllable long and end in a 'hard' consonant [**b, d, f, k, p, s, t, v**] form the plural by adding the ending **-ovi**.

grad	**gradovi**	*city/cities*

Masculine nouns that are one syllable long and end in a 'soft' consonant [**j, lj, nj, c, ć, č, š, dž, đ**] form the plural by adding the ending **-evi**.

miš	**miševi**	*mouse/mice*

Masculine nouns that end in the consonant **-k** form the plural by changing the final consonant into **-c** before adding the plural ending **-i**.

otok	**otoci**	*island(s)*

Some masculine nouns end in **-o**. They form the plural by changing the **-o** to **-i**.

auto	**auti**	*car(s)*

Some nouns have an irregular plural:

čovjek	**ljudi**	*man/men*
dijete	**djeca**	*child/children*

Articles

In Croatian nouns are not preceded by an article such as 'a' or 'the' as they are in English. Thus, *tramvaj* may mean 'streetcar', 'a streetcar' or 'the streetcar'.

The Declension of Nouns

Croatian is an inflected language which means that the nouns and adjectives change their endings depending on the context in which they are used. The special forms belong to different categories which are called 'cases'. Nouns require various changes in the vowels, consonants or endings for each case. There are seven cases in the singular and seven cases in the plural for each Croatian noun. Since there are no comparable changes in English, it may take some time to learn these changes.

Throughout the book we have provided the correct grammatical form for each noun. Don't be too concerned when you are speaking Croatian. You will be understood even if you use the basic nouns provided in the dictionary without making any changes for the cases. However, for those who would like a brief overview of noun declensions, we provide the most basic information below:

Nominative Case

The nominative case is used when the noun is the subject of a sentence.

> **Moja prtljaga nije stigla.**
> *My luggage has not arrived.*

Vocative Case

The vocative case is used when addressing people or objects. It is especially important when using the names and titles of those one wishes to speak to.

> **Gdje je Ivan?**   *Where is Ivan?*   [Nominative case]
> but
> **Ivane, gdje si?**   *Ivan, where are you?*   [Vocative case]

Accusative Case

The accusative case is used when the noun is the direct object of the sentence.

> **Donesite *prtljagu* u moju sobu.**
> *Bring **the luggage** to my room.*

It is also used after some prepositions which denote motion or direction: **kroz**/through, **pod**/under, **pred**/in front of, **u**/in, **niz**/down, and **na**/on.

> **Morate ići kroz *šumu*.**
> *You must go through **the woods**.*

Genitive Case

The genitive case is used to show possession or a relation which is usually expressed in English with *of*.

> ***Ivanova* prtljaga.**
> ***Ivan's** luggage [The luggage **of Ivan**.]*

It is also used after some prepositions such as **od**/from, **bez**/without, **iza**/behind, **blizu**/near, **do**/to.

> **Nije daleko *od hotela*.**
> *It is not far **from the hotel**.*

The genitive is also used after the words **evo** (here is) and **eno** (there is); adverbs of quantity **koliko**/how many, **nekoliko**/some, **mnogo**/many, **malo**/little or few; and nouns of measure **litra**/liter, **kilogram**/a kilo of, **komad**/a piece of.

> **Eno** *hotel.*
> *There's **the hotel**.*
> **Dva komada** *mesa.*
> *Two pieces **of meat**.*
> **Tri litre** *vina.*
> *Three liters **of wine**.*

Dative Case

The dative case is used for the indirect object of an action, and is usually expressed in English with the preposition *to*.

> **Dat ću novce** *blagajniku.*
> *I'll give the money **to the cashier**.*

Instrumental Case

The instrumental case is used for the agent or means by which an action is accomplished. In English this is usually expressed by using the prepositions *with* and *by*. It is also used to express being with or in the company of others.

> **Napisat ću pismo** *olovkom.*
> *I'll write the letter **with a pencil**.*
> **Idem s** *prijateljem.*
> *I'm going **wih a friend**.*

Locative Case

The locative case is used after prepositions which denote location.

> U **Zagrebu.**   *In Zagreb.*
> **na brodu**   *on the boat*
> **u knjizi**   *in the book*

Case Endings

The following tables show the endings which are characteristic for each type of noun in each of the cases.

Masculine Nouns

Inanimate masc.		Animate masc.	
Singular	*Plural*	*Singular*	*Plural*
N hotel	hoteli	prijatelj	prijatelji
V hotele	hoteli	prijatelju	prijatelji
A hotel*	hotele	prijatelja*	prijatelje
G hotela	hotela	prijatelja	prijatelja
D hotelu	hotelima	prijatelju	prijateljima
I hotelom	hotelima	prijateljem	prijateljima
L hotelu	hotelima	prijatelju	prijateljima
Singular	*Plural*	*Singular*	*Plural*
N grad	gradovi	jež	ježevi
V grade	gradovi	ježe	ježevi
A grad	gradove	ježa	ježeve
G grad	gradova	ježa	ježeva
D gradu	gradovima	ježu	ježevima
I gradom	gradovima	ježem	ježevima
L gradu	gradovima	ježu	ježevima

*The accusative singular is the same as nominative for inanimate objects, and the same as genitive for animate objects.

Feminine Nouns

Singular	*Plural*	*Singular*	*Plural*
N knjiga	knjige	N noć	N noći
V knjigo	knjige	V noći	V noći
A knjigu	knjige	A noć	A noći
G knjige	knjiga	G noći	G noći
D knjizi*	knjigama	D noći	D noćima
I knjigom	knjigama	I noći	I noćima
L knjizi*	knjigama	L noći	L noćima

*In forming the dative and locative singular forms, feminine nouns which end in **-ga**, **-ka** and **-ha** change the endings to **-zi**, **-ci** and **-si** respectively.

Neuter Nouns

Singular	Plural	Singular	Plural
N selo	sela	N more	mora
V selo	sela	V more	mora
A selo	sela	A more	mora
G sela	sela	G mora	mora
D selu	selima	D moru	morima
I selom	selima	I morem	morima
L selu	selima	L moru	morima

When travelling you will often use Croatian placenames. Below are the endings to use when saying you are going *to*, coming *from* or are *in* a place.

Placename ending in -a

	to...	*from...*	*in...*
	u...	iz...	u...
Hrvatska	Hrvatsku	Hrvatske	Hrvatskoj
Dalmacija	Dalmaciju	Dalmacije	Dalmaciji
Istra	Istru	Istre	Istri
Amerika	Ameriku	Amerike	Americi
Kanada	Kanadu	Kanade	Kanadi

Placename ending in a consonant.

	to...	*from...*	*in...*
	u...	iz...	u...
Omiš	Omiš	Omiša	Omišu
Sinj	Sinj	Sinja	Sinju
Zagreb	Zagreb	Zagreba	Zagrebu
Frankfurt	Frankfurt	Frankfurta	Frankfurtu

Adjectives

Adjectives generally precede the noun that they modify and they agree in number, gender and case with the noun. In addition, Croatian has two types of adjectives–definite and indefinite. The dictionary at the back of this book contains the indefinite form of masculine adjectives. The definite form of the adjective is generally used before the noun it modifies, while the definite form generally follows the noun.

> **Ovaj visoki čovjek je mlad.** *This tall man is young.*
> **Ovaj mladi čovjek je visok.** *This young man is tall.*

The distinction between the definite and indefinite adjectives is often blurred in everyday speech. Therefore, using the preferred definite form will allow you to be understood in most situations.

Feminine and neuter adjectives are formed by adding the endings **-a** and **-o** respectively to the indefinite masculine form.

mlad	**mlada žena**	*young woman*
velik	**veliko brdo**	*large hill*

Plurals of adjectives are formed by adding the ending **-i** for masculine adjectives, **-e** for feminine adjectives and **-a** for neuter adjectives to the masculine indefinite form.

mlad	**mladi ljudi**	*young people*
mlad	**mlade žene**	*young women*
velik	**velika brda**	*large hills*

The following chart shows the declension of regular adjectives in Croatian.

Declension of adjectives

	masc. sing.	fem. sing.	neut. sing.	masc. pl.	fem. pl.	neut. pl.
N	mlad, mladi	mlada	mlado	mladi	mlade	mlada
V	mladi	mlada	mlado	mladi	mlade	mlada
A	mladi, mladog	mladu	mlado	mlade	mlade	mlada
G	mladog	mlade	mladog	mladih	mladih	mladih
D	mladom	mladoj	mladom	mladim	mladim	mladim
I	mladim	mladom	mladim	mladim	mladim	mladim
L	mladom	mladoj	mladom	mladim	mladim	mladim

Comparative Adjectives

Comparative adjectives are usually derived from the 'positive' form of the adjective by adding the endings **-iji, -ija,** and **-ije** to the masculine indefinite form to produce the masculine, feminine and neuter comparative forms respectively. The masculine comparative adjectives remain the same. The feminine plural is formed by changing the ending to **-ije** and the neuter form by changing the ending to **-ija**.

Sing.	old	masc.	fem.	neuter
	star-	stariji	starija	starije
Plural				
	star-	stariji	starije	starija

Superlative Adjectives

Superlative adjectives are formed by adding the prefix **naj-** to the comparative:

Possessive Adjectives

The following are the possessive adjectives in Croatian:

moj	my	**naš**	our
tvoj	your (sg.)	**Vaš**	your (pl.)
njegov	his	**their**	njihov
njen	her		

Like other adjectives, possessive adjectives must agree in gender, number and case with the noun that they modify.

PERSONAL PRONOUNS

The following chart gives the declension of Croatian personal pronouns:

Singular

N	ja	ti	on	ona	ono
A	me(ne)	te(be)	(nje)ga	(n)ju, je	(nje)ga
G	me(ne)	te(be)	(nje)ga	(n)je	(nje)ga
D	m(en)i	t(eb)i	(nje)mu	n(joj)	(nje)mu
I	mnom	tobom	njim(e)	njom(e)	(nji)me
L	meni	tebi	njemu	njoj	njemu

Plural

N	mi	Vi	oni, one, ona
A	nas	Vas	(nj)ih
G	nas	Vas	(nj)ih
D	nam(a)	Vam(a)	(nj)im
I	nama	Vama	njima
L	nama	Vama	njima

Personal pronouns often have a short form and a long form. The long form is used at the beginning of a sentence, for emphasis and after prepositions. The short form is used the rest of the time. For example:

Ja sam *joj* dao knjigu.   *I gave **her** the book.*
   but
Njoj sam dao knjigu.   *I gave the book **to her**.*

Croatian often omits the personal pronoun when it is the subject of a sentence.

> **Ne ide.**   *He/she/it is not going.*
> **Idem.**   *I'm going.*

However, the pronoun is always used for emphasis.
> **Ona ne ide, ali ja sigurno idem.**
> *She's not going, but I'm going for sure.*

The Personal Pronoun YOU.

Croatian has two forms of the pronoun *you; ti* and *Vi*. *Ti* is a familiar form used for addressing a child, a relative, a close friend. *Vi* is used as the plural form of *you* and as a formal form when addressing persons that one does not know well or that one wishes to show respect toward. The verbs that go with the pronoun *Vi* are always in the plural form.

Interrogative Pronouns

The interrogative pronouns **tko** (who), and **što** (what) and the words **ništa** (nothing), **netko** (someone) and **nitko** (nobody) are declined as follows:

N	(ne)tko	(ne)što
A	(ne)koga	(ne)što
G	(ne)koga	(ne)čega
D	(ne)kome	(ne)čemu
I	(ne)kim(e)	(ne)čim(e)
L	(ne)kome	(ne)čemu

Demonstrative Pronouns

This	**Ovo**	That	**Ono**
These	**Ovi**	Those	**Oni**

The demonstrative pronouns are declined as follows in Croatian:

masc. sing.	fem. sing.	neut. sing.	masc. pl.	fem. pl.	neut. pl.
N ovaj	ova	ovo	ovi	ove	ova
A ovaj, ovog	ovu	ovo	ove	ove	ova
G ovog(a)	ove	ovog(a)	ovih	ovih	ovih
D ovom(e)	ovoj	ovom(e)	ovim(a)	ovim(a)	ovim(a)
I ovom(e)	ovom	ovim(e)	ovim(a)	ovim(a)	ovim(a)
L ovom(e)	ovoj	ovom(e)	ovim(a)	ovim(a)	ovim(a)

Questions

Yes/no questions are formed in Croatian by reversing the word order and adding the question particle **li** after the verb.

You are coming.	*Are you coming?*
Vi dolazite.	**Dolazite li Vi?**

Another simple way to make yes/no questions is to add the words **je li** to a statement with rising intonation to the **je li.**

She came yesterday.	*Did she come yesterday?*
Ona je došla jučer.	**Je li ona došla jučer?**

Verbs

To Be

Present Tense	Affirmative	Negative
I am	**ja sam**	**ja nisam**
you are	**ti si**	**ti nisi**
he is	**on je**	**on nije**

she is	ona je	ona nije
it is	ono je	ono nije
we are	mi smo	mi nismo
you are	Vi ste	Vi niste
they are (m.)	oni su	oni nisu
they are (f.)	one su	one nisu

To Be

Past Tense	Affirmative	Negative
I was	bio sam	(ja) nisam bio
you were	bio si	(ti) nisi bio
he was	bio je	(on) nije bio
she was	bila je	(ona) nije bila
it was	bilo je	ono nije bilo
we were	bili smo	(mi) nismo bili
you were	bili ste	(Vi) niste bili
they were (m.)	bili su	(oni) nisu bili
they were (f.)	bile su	(one) nisu bile

To Be

Future Tense	Affirmative	Negative
I will be	bit ću	(ja) neću biti
you will be	bit ćeš	(ti) nećeš biti
he will be	bit će	(on) neće biti
she will be	bit će	(ona) neće biti
it will be	bit će	(ono) neće biti
we will be	bit ćemo	(mi) nećemo biti
you will be	bit ćete	(Vi) nećete biti
they will be (m.)	bit će	(oni) neće biti
they will be (f.)	bit će	(one) neće biti

To Have

Present Tense	Affirmative	Negative
I have	(ja) imam	(ja) nemam
you have	(ti) imaš	(ti) nemaš
he has	(on) ima	(on) nema

she has	(ona) ima	(ona) nema
it has	(ono) ima	(ono) nema
we have	(mi) imamo	(mi) nemamo
you have	(Vi) imate	(Vi) nemate
they have (m.)	(oni) imaju	(oni) nemaju
they have (f.)	(one) imaju	(one) nemaju

Often personal pronouns are only used in Croatian for emphasis. They have been placed in brackets because they can be omitted in most instances.

Regular Present Tense Verbs

Using the third person singular form of a verb as a base, the following endings are added to form the present tense of Croatian verbs:

ja	---m	mi	---mo
ti	---š	Vi	---te
on/ona/ono	---	oni/one	---e or --u

To Go

ja	idem	mi	idemo
ti	ideš	Vi	idete
on/ona/ono	ide	oni/one	idu

To Ask

(ja) pitam	(mi) pitamo
(ti) pitaš	(Vi) pitate
(on/ona) pita	(oni/one) pitaju

Past Tense

The past tense is formed by selecting the appropriate form of the verb **to be (biti)** and adding an adjective form based on the infinitive.

I asked	**ja sam pitao/pitala**
You asked	**ti si pitao/pitala**

He asked	**on je pitao**
She asked	**ona je pitala**
We asked	**mi smo pitali**
You asked	**Vi ste pitali**
They asked	**Oni su pitali**
They asked	**One su pitale**

To form the past tense adjective, take an infinitive such as **pitati** above, remove the final **-ti** and add **-o** for masculine singular forms, **-li** for masculine plural forms, **-la** for feminine singular forms and **-le** for feminine plural forms.

Future Tense

To express actions which will occur in future time, take the present form of the verb **htjeti** and add an infinitive.

I will travel	**ja ću putovati**
you will travel	**ti ćeš putovati**
he/she will travel	**on/ona će putovati**
we will travel	**mi ćemo putovati**
you will travel	**Vi ćete putovati**
they will travel	**oni/one će putovati**

Since word order is not as strict in Croatian as it is in English, the infinitive can and usually does appear before the helping verb. In this case, the infinitive drops the final **-i**. Instead of **putovati ću,** we get **putovat ću.**

I will travel	**putovat ću**
you will travel	**putovat ćeš**
he/she will travel	**putovat će**
we will travel	**putovat ćemo**
you will travel	**putovat ćete**
they will travel	**putovat će**

The past tense negative is expressed by using the negative of the verb **htjeti** and adding the infinitive:

I will not travel	**(ja) neću putovati**
you will not travel	**(ti) nećeš putovati**
he/she will not travel	**(on/ona) neće putovati**
we will not travel	**(mi nećemo) putovati**
you will not travel	**(Vi) nećete putovati**
they will not travel	**(oni/one) neće putovati**

ENGLISH-CROATIAN
DICTIONARY

A

a jedan
able, to be moći
about o, okolo
above iznad; nad
abroad u inozemstvu
abscess apsces
absolutely apsolutno
accelorator pedala gasa
accept, to primiti, prihvatiti
accident nesreća, nesretan slučaj
accomodations smještaj
accompany, to pratiti
account račun
according to prema
accurate točan
ache bol
across preko
acquaintance poznanik
act, to postupati
actor glumac
actress glumica
adaptor *(elec.)* adapter
add, to dodati
add up, to zbrojiti
address adresa, prebivalište
address book adresar
adjust, to podesiti
admire, to diviti se
admission ulaz
admission ticket ulaznica
admit, to dozvoliti pristup
adore obožavati
Adriatic Sea Jadransko more
adult *(adj.)* odrastao
advance, in unaprijed
adventure avantura; pustolovina
advertisement oglas
advise, to savjetovati
affluent imućan
afraid, to be bojati se
after poslije; nakon
afternoon poslije podne

aftershave losion za brijanje
afterwards kasnije
again opet, ponovo
against protiv
age starost, dob(a)
agency agencija
aggressive agresivan
agree, to pristati; složiti se
AIDS SIDA
air zrak
    air conditioning klimatizacija
    air mattress zračni madrac
airfield zračna luka
airmail zračna pošta
airmail, by zračnom poštom
airplane zrakoplov; avion
airport uzletište; aerodrom
à la carte po narudžbi
alarm uzbuna
alarm clock budilica
alcohol alkohol
alcoholic alkoholičar
alas nažalost
alive živ
all svi; sav; cijeli
all inclusive
    sve je uključeno
all kinds of things
    svega i svačega
allergic alergičan
allergy alergija
alley prolaz
allowed dozvoljen
almost skoro
alone sam
along uz, pokraj
Alps Alpe
already već
also također
alteration izmjena
alternative alternativa
alternator alternator
although iako
altogether sveukupno

always uvijek
a.m. ujutro
amazing začuđujući
ambassador ambasador, poslanik
ambulance kola hitne pomoći
America Amerika
American Amerikanac, američki
among među
amount iznos, suma, svota
amuse oneself, to zabaviti se
amusement razonoda
ancestor predak
anchor sidro
anchovies sardelice
ancient drevan
and i
anesthetic anestetik
angel anđeo
angina angina
angry ljut
angry, to be ljutiti se
animal zvijer
ankle članak
annoy, to smetati (nekome)
another (one) drugi
answer odgovor
answer, to odgovoriti
ant mrav
antagonism antagonizam
antibiotic antibiotik
antifreeze antifriz
antihistamine antihistminik
antique antikni
antique (object) antikni (predmet)
antique shop antikvarijat
antisocial nedruštven
any bilo koji
any time bilo kada
anybody bilo tko
anyhow ipak; bilo kako
anymore više
anyone bilo tko
anything bilo što
apartment stan

apartment house
   stambena zgrada
aperitif aperitiv
apologize, to ispričati se
apology isprika
apothecary ljekarna
appalling užasan
apparatus aparat
appear, to izgledati
appendicitis upala slijepog crijeva
appetite tek, apetit
   bon appétit! dobar tek! u slast!
apple jabuka
apple cake kolač od jabuka
apple pie pita od jabuka
applesauce umak od jabuka
application form obrazac molbe
apply, to podnijeti molbu
appointment sastanak
appreciate, to biti zahvalan
   I appreciate it. Ja sam zahvalan.
approach, to prići
approve, to odobriti
approximately otprilike
apricot marelica
April travanj
archeology arheologija
architect arhitekt
architecture arhitektura
area područje
area code pozivni broj
arm ruka
army vojska
around oko, okolo
arrangements, to make srediti (što)
arrested, to be biti uhapšen
arrival dolazak
arrive, to doći
art umjetnost
art gallery galerija umjetnosti
arthritis artritis
article predmet, artikl
artificial umjetan
artist umjetnik

artistic umjetnički
as kao
ashore, to go iskrcati se
ashtray pepeonik
aside from osim
ask, to pitati
ask for, to tražiti
asleep, to fall zaspati
asparagus šparoga
aspirin aspirin
assault napadaj
assistant pomoćnik
assorted razno
assume, to pretpostaviti
asthma astma
astonishing zapanjujući
at u, na, pred
Atlantic Atlantik
atmosphere atmosfera
attempt pokušaj
attempt, to pokušati
attend, to prisustvovati
attend to, to pobrinuti se za
attorney odvjetnik
attractive privlačan, zgodan
auction dražba, licitacija
audience publika
August kolovoz
aunt teta, ujna, strina
Australia Australija
Australian Australijanac, australski
Austria Austria
Austrian Austrijanac, austrijski
authorities vlasti
automatic automatski
automobile auto, kola
auto trip putovanje autom
autumn jesen
available dostupan
  to be available koji se može dobiti,
   nabaviti
avenue avenija
average prosječan
avoid, to izbjeći

awake budan
away odsutan
awful grozan, strašan
awhile kratko vrijeme
axe sjekira
axle osovina

B

baby beba
baby sitter osoba koja čuva djecu
baby carrier nosiljka za bebu
bachelor neženja
back *(body part)* leđa
back *(rear)* stražnji
  back door stražnja vrata
  in the back otraga
  back seat stražnje sjedište
backache bol u leđima
backpack ruksak
bacon slanina
bad loš
badly loše
bad luck nesreća
bag torba
baggage prtljaga
baggage allowance dozvoljena težina
  prtljage
baggage checkroom garderoba
baggage compartment odioza prtljagu
baggage label natpis na prtljazi
bakery pekara
balcony balkon
bald ćelav
band *(musical)* orkestar
bandage zavoj
bandaid flaster
bank banka
bank account bankovni račun
banquet banket
bar bar, kavić
barber brijač
barber shop brijačnica
barmaid konobarica
bartender barmen

barrette kopča za kosu
basic osnovni
basket košara
bath kupanje
  Can I take a bath?
    Mogu li se okupati?
bath towel ručnik za kupanje
bathing suit kupaći kostim
bathing trunks kupaće gaće
bathrobe ogrtač za kupanje
bathroom kupaonica
bay zaljev
be, to biti
beach plaža
beach umbrella suncobran
bean(s) grah
bear medvjed
beard brada
beat, to pobjediti nad
beautiful lijep
beauty ljepota
beauty salon kozmetički salon
because jer
because of zbog
become, to postati
bed krevet
bed and breakfast noćenje s doručkom
bed linen posteljina
bedroom spavaća soba
bee pčela
beef govedina
beer pivo
before prije
beg, to prositi
begin, to početi
beginning početak
behavior ponašanje
behind iza
beige bež
believe, to vjerovati
bell zvono
belong, to pripadati
belongings imovina
below ispod

belt remen
bend, to sagnuti se
berth ležaj
beside uz; pokraj
besides osim
best najbolji
bet oklada
better bolji
between između
beyond iza
beverage piće
bicycle kotur, bicikl
big velik
bigger veći
biggest najveći
bill račun
billfold novčarka
billiards bilijar
bird ptica
birthday rođendan
biscuit keks
bit malo
bite ugriz
bite, to ugristi
bitter gorak
black crn
blackout, to have a onesvijestiti se
bladder mjehur
blank prazan
blanket deka
blazer sako
bleach bjelilo
bleak pust
bleed, to krvariti
bless, to blagosloviti
Bless you! Nazdravlje!
blessing blagoslov
blind slijep
blind spot slijepa točka
blister žulj
blocked blokiran
blonde plavuša
blood krv
bloody krvav

blouse bluza
blue plav
blusher rumenilo
board daska, ploča
board, full puni pansion
boat brod
body tijelo
boil, to kipjeti
boil *(on body)* čir
bomb bomba
bone kost
book knjiga
bookstore knjižara
boot čizma
booze alkoholno piće
border granica
boring dosadan
born rođen
borrow, to posuditi
boss šef
both oboje
bother, to smetati
bottle boca
bottle opener otvarač za boce
bottom dno
  from the bottom iz dna
bouncer izbacivač
bowling kuglanje
bowling alley kuglana
box kutija
box office kazališna blagajna
boy dječak
boyfriend dečko
bra grudnjak
bracelet narukvica
brake kočnica
branch grana
brandy rakija
brassiere grudnjak
brave hrabar
bread kruh
bread and butter kruh s maslacem
break, to slomiti
breakfast doručak

breath dah
breathe, to disati
breeze povjetarac
breezy svjež
brick cigla
bridal suite apartman za mladence
bride nevjesta
bridegroom mladoženja
bridge most
brief kratak
briefcase aktovka
bright sjajan
brim rub
bring, to donijeti
bring along, to ponijeti sa sobom
Britain Britanija
brochure brošura
broad široki
broken slomljen
brooch broš
brother brat
brother-in-law šurjak
brown smeđ
bruise modrica
brunette *(woman)* crnka
brush četka
bucket vedro
buffet bife
bug kukac
buckle up, to zakopčati
build, to (sa)graditi
build up, to izgraditi
building zgrada
bulb (light) žarulja
bump, to udariti
bumper *(auto)* odbojnik
bunk ležaj
bun *(roll)* zemička
buoy plovak
burglar provalnik
burgundy *(color)* bordo
burgundy *(wine)* burgundac
burn opekotina
burn, to gorjeti

burn oneself, to opeći se
bus autobus
bus station autobusni kolodvor
bus stop autobusna postaja
business posao; trgovina
businessman poslovni čovjek
business card posjetnica
business trip poslovno putovanje
busy *(person)* zaposlen
busy *(place)* prometan
but ali
butcher mesar
butter maslac
butterfly leptir
button dugme
buy, to kupiti
by kraj
  day by day dan za danom
  side by side bok uz bok
by all means svakako
by day danju
by night noću
by now do sad
by oneself sam
by the dozen na tucete
by the time... dok...
bye-bye do viđenja

C

cab taksi
cabaret kabare
cabbage kupus; zelje
cabbage, pickled kiseli kupus, kiselo
zelje
cabbage, stuffed sarma
cabin kabina
  outside cabin vanjska kabina
café kavana, kafić
cage kavez
cake torta
calamity velika nesreća
calculator računar
calendar kalendar

call, to zvati
  to call on posjetiti
  to call up pozvati
calm miran
calories kalorije
camera foto-aparat
camp kamp
camping kampiranje
campsite kampiralište
can konzerva
can *(to be able to)* moći
Canada Kanada
Canadian Kanađanin, kanadski
cancel, to otkazati
cancellation otkaz
candies bomboni
candle svijeća
canoe kanu
can opener, otvarač za konzerve
capital *(money)* kapital
capital *(city)* glavni grad
capital letters, velika slova
capsize, to prevrnuti se
captain kapetan
car auto
  car ferry trajekt
carbonated (drink) gazirano (piće)
card karta
cardboard box kartonska kutija
cardigan vesta, džemper
carefree bezbrižan
careful pažljiv, oprezan
careless nemaran
carnation karanfil
carnival *(mardi gras)* poklade
carp šaran
carpet tepih
carrot mrkva
carry, to nositi
carry away, to odnijeti
carry over, to prenijeti
carton karton
carton of cigarettes kutija cigareta
case *(suitcase)* kovčeg

case slučaj
  in any case u svakom slučaju
  in case u slučaju
cash novac, gotovina
casino kasino
cassette kazeta
castle kula
casual (clothes) sportska (odjeća)
cat mačka
catamaran splav
catalog katalog
catch, to uhvatiti
cathedral katedrala
Catholic Katolik; katolički
cauliflower cvjetača
cause uzrok
caution opreznost
cave špilja
caviar ikra, kavijar
ceiling strop
celebration proslava
celery celer
cellophane celofan
celsius celzij
cemetary groblje
center centar; sredina
centigrade celzij
centimeter centimetar
central srednji, glavni
century stoljeće
ceramics keramika
certain siguran
certainly sigurno
certificate potvrda
chain lanac
chair stolica
  deck-chair ležaljka
  easy chair fotelja
chambermaid sobarica
champagne šampanjac
chance slučaj
change (money) sitniš
change, to promijeniti
change for, to zamijeniti

channel kanal
chapel kapela
character karakter
charge, to naplatiti
charge, to (on a credit card)
  staviti na kreditnu karticu
charge, to be in biti odgovoran
charge card kreditna kartica
charm čar
charming (person) šarmantan
charming (place or thing) čaroban
chassis šasija
chat, to pričati
cheap jeftin
cheat, to prevariti
check (monetary) ček
check (bill) račun
check, to provjeriti
  check the luggage, to predati prtljagu
  check in, to prijaviti se (u hotel)
checkers (game) dame
cheek obraz
cheerful veseo
cheerfulness veselje
cheers živjeli
cheese sir
cheesecake kolač od sira
chef [glavni] kuhar
chemical kemijski
chemist (pharmacist) ljekarnik
cherry trešnja
chess šah
chest grudi
chewing gum žvakaća guma
chicken pile(tina)
  chicken soup pileća juha
  fried chicken pohana piletina
  roast chicken pečena piletina
chickenpox kozice
chief glavni
child dijete
childhood djetinstvo
children djeca
children's dječji

chilled ohlađen
chilly hladno
chimney dimnjak
chin brada
china porculan
China Kina
Chinese Kinez, kineski
chips čips, pomfrit
chocolate čokolada
choke *(auto)* čok
choose, to izabrati
chop *(meat)* odrezak
Christmas Božić
  Merry Christmas Sretan Božić
church crkva
cider jabukovača
cigar cigara
cigarette cigareta
cinema kino
circle krug
citizen građanin, državljanin
city grad
city center centar grada
city hall gradska vijećnica
clarify razjasniti
class razred
classical klasičan
clean čist
clean, to čistiti
cleansing cream krema za čišćenje
  lica
clear jasno
climate klima
climb, to penjati se
climbing boots planinske cipele
clinic klinika
clip kopča
cloakroom garderoba
clock sat
close blizu
close, to zatvoriti
closed zatvoren
closet ormar
clothes odjeća

cloud oblak
  cloudy, to be biti oblačno
club klub
clutch kvačilo
coach *(bus)* autobus
coarse grub
coast obala
coastguard obalna straža
coat kaput
coat hanger vješalica
cockroach žohar
cocktail koktel
coffee kava
coins kovani novac
coincidence slučajnost
cold hladan
  it's cold hladno je
cold cream krema za lice
cold cuts hladno jelo
collapse, to srušiti se
collar ovratnik
colleague kolega
collect *(call)* poziv na njihov račun
collect, to sakupljati
college visoka škola
collision sudar
color boja
comb češalj
comb, to češljati
combination kombinacija
combine, to kombinirati
come, to doći
  come close to, to približiti se
  come off, to otpasti
  come out, to izići
come in! uđite!
comfort komfor
comfortable udoban
commodity roba
common običan
common, in zajednički
common market zajedničko europsko
  tržište
company *(commercial)* poduzeće

company *(guests)* gosti
comparison usporedba
compartment odio
compartment *(train)* kupe
compass busola
compassion samilost
complain, to žaliti se
complaint žalba
complete potpun
complete, to dopuniti, dovršiti
completely sasvim
complicated komplicirano
compliment kompliment
compose, to skladati
composer skladatelj
compositon djelo
computer računalo, kompjuter
concerned, to be biti zabrinut
concert koncert
concussion potres mozga
condenser *(auto)* kondenzator
condition stanje
conditioner *(hair)* regenerator
condom prezervativ, kondom
conductor kondukter
conference konferencija, vijećanje
confirm, to potvrditi
confess, to priznati
conflict sukob
confuse, to zbuniti
congratulate, to čestitati (nekome)
   I congratulate you čestitam Vam
Congratulations! čestitam
conjunctivitis konjunktivitis
connect, to spojiti; biti u vezi
connection veza
connoisseur vještak
conquer, to pobijediti
conscious pri svijesti
conservative konzervativan
constipation konstipacija
construct, to sagraditi
consul konzul
consulate konzulat

contact dodir, veza
contact, to stupiti u vezu
contact lenses kontaktne leće
contemporary suvremen
content zadovoljan
continent kontinent
continue, to nastaviti
contraceptive sredstvo za
   kontracepciju
contract ugovor
contribute, to doprinijeti
control, to kontrolirati
controversial polemički
convenient pogodan
cook kuhar(ica)
cook, to kuhati
cookie sitni kolač; keks
cool *(weather)* svježe
copy kopija
copy, to kopirati
cordial srdačan
corduroy kord-samt
cork čep
corkscrew vadičep
corn kukuruz
cornbread kukuruzni kruh
cornflakes kukuruzne pahuljice
corner ugao
   the house on the corner
   kuća na uglu
coronary infarkt
correct pravilan
correct, to be biti u pravu
corridor hodnik
correspond, to dopisivati se
cosmetics kozmetika
cost cijena
cost, to koštati; stajati
   how much does it cost? koliko
   stoji?
costume nošnja
   native costume narodna nošnja
cot poljski krevet
cotton pamuk

cotton balls loptice od vate
couch kauč
couchette kušet
cough kašalj
cough syrup sirup za kašalj
count brojiti
  please count it molim Vas prebrojite
country država
country, in the izvan grada
couple par
  a couple of... nekoliko...
course *(school)* tečaj
course *(of meal)* jelo
  of course naravno
court *(law)* sud
court *(game)* igralište
cousin *(male)* bratić, rođak
cousin *(female)* sestrična, rođakinja
cover, to pokriti
cover charge doplatak
cow krava
cozy udoban
crab rak
cracked puknut
cracker slani keks
crafts rukotvorine
cramp grč
crankshaft radilica
crash sudar
crate, to staviti u sanduk
crawl, to puzati
crazy lud
cream krema, vrhnje
  whipped cream tučeno vrhnje
credit card kreditna kartica
crib dječji krevetić
crisis kriza
Croat *see Croatian*
Croatia Hrvatska
Croatian Hrvat(ica), hrvatsko
crook lopov
cross, to preći
crossing prijelaz
crossroads raskrsnica

crowd mnoštvo
crowded prometan, prepun
crown kruna
crucial neophodan
cruise krstarenje
crutch štaka
cry, to vikati, plakati
cucumber krastavac
cuff manšeta
cuisine kuharstvo, kuhinja
cultural kulturan
culture kultura
cup šalica
cupboard ormar
cure, to izliječiti
curlers *(hair)* vitleri
currency valuta, novac
currency, hard devize
current aktualan
curtain zavjesa
cushion pillow
custom običaj
custom-made po narudžbi
customs carina
customs declaration carinska izjava
customs examination carinski pregled
customs officer carinik
cut, to rezati
cute zgodan
cutlery pribor za jelo
cutlets odresci
cylinder cilindar
cystisis cistitis

D

Dalmatia Dalmacija
Dalmatian Dalmatinac, dalmatinski
damage šteta
damage, to oštetiti
damaged oštećeno
damp vlažan
dance ples
dance, to plesati
dancer plesač(ica)

dandruff perut
danger opasnost
dangerous opasan
dare, to usuditi se
dark taman
dark, to get smračiti se
dashboard šoferska ploča
date *(fruit)* datula
date datum
  make a date ugovoriti sastanak
daughter kći
daughter-in-law snaha
dawn zora
day dan
  days, for danima
day trip jednodnevni izlet
dead mrtav
deaf gluh
deal *(business)* posao
  it's a deal ugovoreno
dealer trgovac
dear drag
Dear Sir Cijenjeni gospodine
Dear Madam Cijenjena gospođo
death smrt
December prosinac
decide odlučiti
decision odluka
deck paluba
  deck-chair ležaljka
declare, to *(customs)* prijaviti
decoration ukras
deduct odbiti
deduction odbitak
deep dubok
defeat poraz
defeat, to pobijediti
definite određen
definitely sigurno
degree *(university)* diploma
degree *(temperature)* stupanj
delay odgoda
delay, to odgoditi
delayed, to be kasniti

deliberately namjerno
delicacy specijalitet
delicate nježan
delicious ukusan
deliver, to isporučiti
delivery isporuka
denim traper
Denmark Danska
dental floss konac za čišćenje zubi
denture zubalo
dentist stomatolog; zubar
deny, to poreći
deodorant dezoderans
depart, to otputovati
department odio
department store robna kuća
departure odlazak
depend, to ovisiti
dependable pouzdan
deposit depozit
deposit, to uložiti
depressed potišten
depressed *(area, beach)* pust
depth dubina
description opis
desire želja
desk pisaći stol
dessert poslastica
destroy, to uništiti
detergent deterdžent
detour zaobilazni put
devalued devalviran
develop, to *(film)* razviti (film)
devil vrag
diabetic dijabetičar
dialect narječje, dijalekt
diapers pelene
diarrhea proljev
diary dnevnik
dictate, to diktirati
dictionary rječnik
die, to umrijeti
diesel *(fuel)* dizel
diet dijeta

difference razlika
different različit
difficult težak
difficulty teškoća
dig, to kopati
digestion probava
diner *(car)* vagon-restoran
dining hall blagovaona
dining room blagovaonica
dinner večera
dinner jacket smoking
dipstick mjerač nivoa ulja
direct ravan
direction smjer
directly odmah
directory, telephone telefonski imenik
dirty prljavo
disabled invalid
disappear, to nestati
disappointed, to be biti razočaran
disaster katastrofa
discharge gnoj
disco disko
discount popust
discount, to sniziti cijenu
disease bolest
disgusting odvratan
dish *(meal)* jelo
dish *(plate)* tanjur, posuda
dishcloth krpa za pranje posuđa
dislocated iščašeno
dissatisfied nezadovoljan
dissolve, to rastopiti
distance daljina
  in the distance u daljini
distilled water distilirana voda
distress nevolja
distributor *(auto)* razvodnik
disturb, to smetati
ditch jarak
divine božanski
diving board daska za skakanje u vodu
divorced razveden

dizzy, to feel imati vrtoglavicu
do, to raditi, (u)činiti
  What shall we do tonight?
  Što ćemo raditi večeras?
dock pristanište
doctor liječnik
document dokument
dog pas
doll lutka
dollar dolar
donkey magarac
don't nemoj(te)
door vrata
dosage doza
dot točka
doughnut krafna
dove golub
down *(feathers)* perje
  down comforter perina
down dolje
downstairs dolje
  to go downstairs ići dolje
downward prema dolje
dozen tucet
drain odvodna cijev
drapes zavjese
draw, to crtati
drawer ladica
dream san
dream, to sanjati
dress haljina
dress, to obući se
dresser kredenc
dressing *(wound)* zavoj
dressing *(salad)* začin
drink, to piti
drive, to voziti
driver vozač
drug droga, lijek
druggist ljekarnik
drug store ljekarna
during za vrijeme
dwarf patuljak
dye, to bojati

E

each (one) svaki
eagle orao
ear uho
earache, I have an boli me uho
earlier ranije
early rano
earring naušnica
earnest iskren
earth zemlja
east istok
  to the east of... istočno od...
  in the east na istoku
Easter Uskrs
easy lako
eat, to jesti
eatery restoran; gostionica
edible jestiv
efficient efikasan
egg jaje
  fried egg pečeno jaje
  scrambled egg kajgana
eggplant plavi patlidžan
either...or... ili...ili...
elastic elastika
elbow lakat
elect, to izabrati
electric električan
electrical outlet utičnica
electrician električar
electricity struja
elegant elegantan
elephant slon
elevator lift
else drugo
  nothing else, thanks ništa više, hvala
  something else nešto drugo
  somewhere else negdje drugdje
  what else? sto još?
embarrassed, to be biti neugodno (kome)
embassy ambasada, poslanstvo
emergency hitni slučaj

emery board šmirgla
emigrant iseljenik
emotional emocionalan
empire carstvo
empty prazan
enclose, to zatvoriti
encourage, to poticati
end kraj
end, to završiti
energetic energičan
energy energija
engaged *(to be married)* zaručen
engaged *(busy)* zauzet
engine motor
England Engleska
English engleski
Englishman Englez
Englishwoman Engleskinja
engraver rezbar; graver
enjoy, to uživati
enlargement (of photo) povećanje
enormous ogroman
enough dovoljno
  that's enough dosta je
enter, to ući
entertainment zabava
entire cijelo
entrance ulaz
entrust oneself, to vjerovati (kome)
envelope omotnica, kuverta
epileptic epileptičar
equal ravnopravan
equality ravnopravnost
equipment oprema
erotic erotičan
error greška
especially naročito
espresso coffee espresso
essential bitno
ethnic *(clothing, crafts)* narodni
Europe Europa
European europski
even čak
evening večer

eventually konačno
ever ikada
every svaki
everybody svatko
everyone svatko
everything sve
everywhere svuda
evil zlo
exactly točno
examine, to pregledati
examination *(medical)* pregled
examination *(test)* ispit
example primjer
  for example na primjer
excellent izvrstan
  excellent! izvrmso!
except osim
exception izuzetak
exchange, to izmijeniti
excited uzbuđen
excursion izlet
excuse izgovor
excuse, to ispričati; oprostiti
excuse me oprostite
exert, to napregnuti
exhaust *(auto)* ispušna cijev
exhausted iscrpljen
exhibition izložba
exist, to postojati
exit izlaz
exit, to izići
expect, to očekivati
expensive skup
experience iskustvo
experience, to doživjeti
experienced iskusan
expert stručnjak
expired, it's isteklo je
explain, to objasniti
explanation objašnjenje
export izvoz
export, to izvoziti
exposure meter svjetlomjer
express train brzi vlak

expression izraz
extra dodatni
extraordinary neobičan
extremely krajnje
eye oko
  to keep an eye on pripaziti
eye drops kapi za oči
eye shadow sjenilo za oči
eyebrow obrva
eyebrow pencil olovka za obrve
eyewitness očevidac

F

face lice
fact činjenica
factory tvornica
faint, to onesvijestiti se
fair *(commercial)* sajam
  it's not fair nije pošteno
fall *(season)* jesen
fall, to pasti
  to fall apart raspasti se
  to fall out ispasti
false neistinit; lažan
false teeth umjetni zubi
familiar poznat
family obitelj
family name prezime
famished, to be umirati od glada
famous čuven
fan ventilator
fan *(sports)* navijač
fan belt remen ventilatora
far dalek
  is it far? je li daleko?
farmer seljak
farther dalje
fashion moda
fast brz
fasten, to zakopčati
fastener kopča
fat debeo
fate sudbina
father otac

father-in-law svekar; punac
faucet pipa
fault krivnja
faulty neispravan
fear strah
fear, to bojati se
feather pero
   feather pillow jastuk od perja
February veljača
fee naplata
feel, to osjećati
fellow čovjek
fence ograda
fender branik
ferry trajekt
festival proslava; festival
fetch, to donijeti
fever groznica
few malo
   a few nekoliko
fiance zaručnik, zaručnica
field polje
fifty-fifty pola i pola
fight tuča
fight, to boriti se
fig smokva
figure *(number)* brojka
figure *(person)* oblik; figura
figure, to izračunati
fill, to napuniti
fill, to (a tooth) blombirati
fill out, to ispuniti
fill up, to napuniti
fill up, to *(gasoline)* natenkirati
fillet file
filling *(tooth)* blomba
filling station benzinska postaja
film film
filtar filter
filthy prljav
finally konačno
find, to naći
fine fino
fine *(monetary)* globa, kazna

finger prst
fingernail nokat
finish, to dovršiti
finished gotov
Finland Finska
fire vatra, požar
fire! požar!
fire alarm požarna uzbuna
fire escape požarne stube
fire extinguisher aparat za gašenje
   požara
firm tvrd
firm *(company)* poduzeće
first prvi
   at first najprije
first aid prva pomoć
first aid kit pribor za prvu pomoć
first class prvorazredni
first name ime
firstly najprije
fish riba
fish, to loviti ribu
fish-hook udica
fish market ribarnica
fisherman ribar
fishing ribanje; ribolov
fishing boat ribarski čamac
fishing net mreža za ribanje
fishing rod štap za ribanje
fishing tackle pribor za ribanje
fit, to odgovarati
fit, to be biti u formi
fix, to popraviti
fixed *(repaired)* popravljeno
fixed *(stationary)* nepomičan
fizzy gaziran
flab salo
flag barjak, zastava
flame plamen
flannel flanel
flash *(camera)* blic
flashlight baterija
flat ravan
flat tire ispuhana guma

flavor ukus
fleck mrlja
flea buha
flea powder prašak protiv buha
flee, to bježati
flesh meso
flexible savitljiv
flight *(airplane)* let
flippers peraja
flimsy slab
flood poplava
floor pod
florist cvjećar
flounder *(fish)* iverak
flour brašno
flower cvijet
flu gripa
fluent tečno
flush (a toilet) pustiti vodu
fly muha
fly *(on trousers)* šlic
fly, to letjeti
fog magla
foggy maglovito
fold, to presaviti
folder faksikl
folk costume narodna nošnja
folk customs narodni običaji
folk dance narodni ples
folk music narodna glazba
folk song narodna pjesma
follow, to slijediti
fond, to be (of) voljeti
food hrana
food poisoning otrovanje želuca
food store samoposluga
fool luđak
foolish glup
foot noga
football *(soccer)* nogomet
for za
forbid, to zabraniti
forbidden zabranjen
force, to prisiliti

forehead čelo
foreign stran
foreign exchange devize
foreign language strani jezik
foreigner stranac
forenoon prijepodne
forest šuma
forget, to zaboraviti
forgetful zaboravan
forgive, to oprostiti (kome)
fork vilica
forks and spoons žlice i vilice
form oblik
formal formalan
formerly prije toga
fortification jačanje
fortified pojačano
fortress tvrđava
fotunate sretan
fortunately srećom
fortune teller gatara
forty četrdeset
forward naprijed
founder osnivač
foundation podlog
foundation *(facial)* tekući puder
fountain vodoskok; fontana
fountain pen penkala
four četiri
fourth, a jedna četvrtina
fracture, to slomiti
fragile lomljiv
frame okvir
France Francuska
fraud prijevara
free slobodan
free of charge besplatan
free of customs duty oslobođeno carine
freight teret; tovar
freighter teretni brod
French francuski
Frenchman Francuz
Frenchwoman Francuskinja
French fries pomfrit

frequent čest
fresh svjež
friction trvenje
Friday petak
fried pečen
friend prijatelj(ica)
friendly prijateljski; ljubazan
friendship prijateljstvo
frightened, to be bojati se
frog žaba
from od
from all over od svakale
from it od toga
front prednji
  front of, in ispred
frozen zamrznut
fruit voće
  stewed fruit kuhano voće
fruit juice voćni sok
fruit salad voćna salata
fry, to pržiti
frying pan tava
fulfill, to ispuniti
full pun
fun zabavno
function *(gathering)* društvena priredba
function, to djelovati
funeral pogreb
funny smiješan
furnished namješten
furniture namještaj
further dalje
furthermore osim toga
fuse osigurač
future budućnost

G

gale oluja
gallstone žučni kamenac
gamble, to kockati
game igra
garage garaža
garage *(repair shop)* auto-servis

garden vrt
garlic češnjak
gas plin
gasoline benzin
  gas pedal pedal za gas
  gas station benzinska postaja
  gas tank benzinski rezervoar
gasket brtvilo
gate vrata; kapija
gather, to sakupiti
gauge mjerilo
gay homoseksualan
gear *(mech.)* zupčanici, brzina
gearbox mjenjačka kutija
gearshift poluga mjenjača
gender spol
general sveopći
generous velikodušan
generator generator
gentleman gospodin
genuine pravi
German Njemac, njemački
German measles rubeola
Germany Njemačka
get, to (something) nabaviti (što)
get dressed, to obući se
get by, to proći
get down, to sići
get in, to ući
get off, to *(clothing)* svući
get rid of, to rješiti se (čega)
get to, to doći do
get up, to dići se
ghastly grozan
ghost duh
giant gigant
gift poklon
gigantic ogroman
gin džin
  gin and tonic džin i tonik
girl djevojka
give, to dati
give advice, to savjetovati
give change, to razmijeniti

give in exhange, to zamijeniti
give up, to odustati
give a message, to dati poruku (kome)
glad radostan
glad, to be biti radostan
gladly drage volje
gland žlijezda
glass staklo
glass *(drinking)* čaša
glasses naočale
glassware staklo; staklena roba
glory slava
gloves rukavice
glue ljepilo
gnat mušica
go, to ići
go back, to vratiti se
go by, to proći
go in, to ući
go near, to približiti se
go on, to ići dalje; nastaviti
go out, to izići
go over, to pregledati
goat koza
goat's cheese kozji sir
God Bog
godchild kumče
godfather kum
godmother kuma
gold zlato
gold *(adj.)* zlatan
golf golf
golf club štap za golf
golf course igralište za golf
good dobar
good looking zgodan
goodbye zbogom; do viđenja
goods roba
goose guska
gooseberry ogrozd
gorgeous divan
gourmet poznavalac dobrog jela i pića
government vlada
gradually postupno

grammar gramatika
grand velik
granddaughter unuka
grandfather djed
grandmother baka
grandson unuk
grapefruit grep(frut)
grapefruit juice sok od grepfruta
grapes grožđe
grass trava
grateful zahvalan
gravy umak od mesa
gray siv
grease mast
grease, to podmazati
greasy mastan
great velik
Great Britain Velika Britanija
Greece Grčka
greed lakomost
greedy lakom
Greek Grk, grčki
green zelen
greet, to pozdraviti
grilled sa roštilja
ground *(earth)* zemlja
ground beef mljevena govedina
ground floor prizemlje
group grupa
grown-up odrastao
guarantee garancija
guess, to pogoditi
guest gost
guest room soba za gosta
guide vodič
guidebook vodič
guilty kriv
guitar gitara
gum *(chewing)* žvakaća guma
gums *(dental)* zubni desni
gun vatreno oružje
guy čovjek; momak
gynecologist ginekolog

H

hair kosa
hair dryer fen za kosu
hair dye boja za kosu
hair gel gel za kosu
hair mousse pjena za kosu
hair spray lak za kosu
hairbrush četka za kosu
haircut šišanje
hairdresser frizer
hairdressing salon frizerski salon
half pola
  a half polovica
half-brother polubrat
hall sala
ham šunka
hamburger hamburger
hammer čekić
hand ruka
hand in, to uručiti
hand over, to predati
handbag torba
handbrake ručna kočnica
handkerchief maramica
handle ručka
handmade ručni rad
handsome lijep, zgodan
handwriting rukopis
hang, to visiti
hang up, to *(telephone)*
  spustiti slušalicu
hanger vješalica
hangover, to have a biti mamuran
happen, to dogoditi se
happiness sreća
happy sretan
happy-go-lucky bezbrižan
harbor luka
hard tvrd; težak
hard-boiled egg tvrdo kuhano jaje
hardly jedva
harm šteta
harmful štetan

harmless neopasan
hat šešir
hate mržnja
hate, to mrziti
have, to imati
hay fever peludna groznica
he on
head glava
headache glavobolja
  headache, I have a boli me glava
headlight prednje svijetlo
health zdravlje
healthy zdrav
hear, to čuti
hearing aid slušni aparat
heart srce
heart attack srčani napad
heartily srdačno
heat vrućina
heater grijač
heating grijanje
heaven nebo
heavy težak
heel peta
height visina
helicopter helikopter
helmet kaciga
help pomoć
help, to pomoći
helpful, to be biti od pomoći
hepatitis hepatitis
herbs biljke
hem (po)rub
here ovdje
  here! *(direction to place)* ovamo!
hiccups štucanje
hide, to sakriti
high visok
high chair dječja stolica
highway autoput
hike, to pješačiti
hiking pješačenje
hill brdo
hip kuk

historical povjesni
history povijest
hit, to udariti
hitchhike, to stopirati
hitchhiker autostoper
hold, to držati
hole rupa
holiday blagdan
holy svet
home dom
homemade domaći
homesick nostalgičan za domom
homesickness nostalgija za domom
honest pošten
honey med
honeymoon medeni mjesec
hood *(auto)* hauba
hope nada
hope, to nadati se
hope, I ja se nadam
horn *(auto)* truba
horrible užasan
horrified prestrašen
horse konj
horseback riding jahanje
hospital bolnica
hospitality gostoprimstvo
hot vruć
hot dog hrenovka
hotel hotel
hour sat
house kuća
  at the house of kod
 housewife domaćica
how kako
how many? koliko?
humid sparno
humidity sparina
Hungarian Mađar, mađarski
Hungary Mađarska
hunger glad
hungry gladan
hunt, to loviti
hurry, to žuriti

hurt, to boljeti
husband suprug
hydrofoil hidrogliser

I

I ja
ice led
ice cream sladoled
ice cream cone kornet sladoleda
ice water ledena voda
iced coffee ledena kava
idea ideja
ideal idealan
idiot idiot
identification paper legitimacija
if ako
ignition paljenje
ill bolestan
illegal ilegalan
illegible nečitak
illness bolest
imagine, to maštati
imitation imitacija
immediately odmah
immigrant imigrant
immigration imigracija
import uvoz
import, to uvoziti
importance važnost
important važan
impossible nemoguć
impress, to impresionirati
impression utisak
impressive koji ostavlja dojam
improve, to poboljšati
impulse impuls; pogon
in u
in advance unaprijed
inasmuch ukoliko
include, to uključiti
inconvenient nezgodan
increase, to povećati
incredible nevjerojatan
indecent nepristojan

independent neovisan
India Indija
Indian Indijac, indijski
Indian (American) Indijanac, indijanski
indigestion loša probava
indoor pool zatvoreni bazen
indoors unutra
industry industrija
infection zaraza
infectious zarazan
inflammation upala
inflame, to upaliti
inflation inflacija
influence utjecaj
inform, to obavijestiti, informirati
informal neformalan
information informacije
information desk šalter za informacije
inhabitant stanovnik
injection injekcija
injured povrijeđen
injury povrijeda
ink tinta
innocent nevin
inquisitive radoznao
insane lud
insect kukac
insecticide insekticid
inside unutra
insincere neiskren
insist, to insistirati
insomnia nesanica
instead umjesto
instructive poučan
insulin insulin
insult uvrijeda
insult, to uvrijediti
insurance osiguranje
intellectual intelektualac
intelligent inteligentan
intentional namjeran
interest *(places of)* znamenitost
interest *(financial)* kamate

interesting zanimljiv
international međunarodni
interpret, to tumačiti
interpreter tumač
intersection raskrsnica
interrupt, to prekinuti
into u
introduce, to predstaviti
introduce oneself, to predstaviti se
in vain uzalud
invalid *(adjective)* nevažeći
invalid *(noun)* invalid
investigate, to istraživati
invitation pozivnica
invite, to pozvati
iodine jod
Ireland Irska
Irish irski
iron glačalo
iron, to glačati
is je
island otok
isolated izoliran
it ono
Italian Talijan, talijanski
Italy Italija
itch, to svrbiti
itinerary raspored

⌐

jack *(auto)* dizalica
jacket jakna, sako
jam pekmez, džem
January siječanj
jaundice žutica
jaw vilica
jealous ljubomoran
jeans traperice
jellyfish meduza
jetty molo, pristanište
Jew Židov
jewel dragi kamen
jewelry nakit
Jewish židovski

job posao
jog, to trčati
join, to priključiti se
joint *(anat.)* zglob
joke šala
joke, to šaliti se
journey putovanje
joy radost, sreća
jug bokal
juice sok
July srpanj
jump, to skakati
jumper cables kabl za spajanje akumulatora
June lipanj
just samo, tek
just *(proper)* pravedan
just across odmah preko
just now baš sada
just so baš tako
justice pravosuđe

K

keep, to držati
keep secret, to tajiti
kerosene petrolej
ketchup kečup
key ključ
kid klinac
kidney bubreg
kill, to ubiti
kilo kilogram
kilometer kilometar
kind *(type)* vrsta
kind *(nice)* ljubazan
kiss poljubac
kiss, to poljubiti
kitchen kuhinja
Kleenex papirna maramica
knee koljeno
knap sack ruksak
knife nož
knight vitez
knitting pletenje

knives noževi
knock, to kucati
knot čvor
know, to *(a fact)* znati
know, to *(a person)* poznati
knowledge znanje
known poznat

L

label naljepnica
lace, to žnirati
laces (shoe) uzice
lady gospođa
lake jezero
lamb janjetina
lamb chop janjeći odrezak
lamp lampa
land zemlja
landscape krajolik
language jezik
large velik
laryngitis laringitis
last zadnji
last name prezime
late kasno
   the latest thing najnovije
lately u zadnje vrijeme
later kasnije
laugh, to smijati se
laughter smijeh
laundromat praonica
lavatory zahod
law zakon
lawyer odvjetnik
laxative laksativ
lay, to ležati
lazy lijen
lead, to voditi
leaf list
leaflet prospekt
leak, to curiti
learn, to učiti
least najmanje
least, at barem

least, not in the nimalo
leather koža
leather goods kožni proizvodi
leave, to ostaviti
leave, to *(go away)* otići
lecture predavanje
left lijevo
leg noga
  leg of lamb janjeći but
legal legalan
lemon limun
lemonade limunada
lemon tea čaj s limunom
length dužina
lengthen poduljiti
lens *(photography)* objektiv
lens *(contact)* leća
lent korizma
less manje
lesson lekcija
let, to *(rent)* iznajmiti
let, to *(allow)* dopustiti
letter pismo
lettuce zelena salata
lever ručica
liable odgovoran
library knjižnica
license (driver's) vozačka iskaznica
lid poklopac
lie, to lagati
life život
lifeboat čamac za spasavanje
light svijetlo
light bulb žarulja
light meter svjetlomjer
light, to svijetliti
lighten, to olakšati
lighter upaljač
lighthouse svjetionik
lightning munja
like kao
like, to voljeti
  I would like... želio bih...
limb grana

limited ograničeno
line linija
linen posteljina
lining podstava
lion lav
lip usna
lip brush četkica za usne
lip gloss sjaj za usne
lipstick ruž za usne
liqueur liker
liquor alkoholna pića
list spisak
listen, to slušati
liter litra
litter smeće
little malen
little, a malo
live, to živjeti
lively živo
liver jetra
lizard gušter
living room primaća soba
loaf hljeb
lobby predvorje
lobster jastog
local lokalni
lock brava
locker pretinac
log panj
lonely usamljen
long dug
long-distance call međugradski
  razgovor
look, to gledati
look after, to pripaziti
look around, to gledati okolo
look back, to gledati iza (sebe)
look up, to gledati gore
loose labav
lose, to izgubiti
lotion losion
loud glasan
love ljubav
love, to voljeti

lovely krasan
low nizak
luck sreća
lucky sretan
luggage prtljaga
lumbago lumbago
lumpfish morski okunj
lunch ručak
lungs pluća
luxurious luksuzan
luxury luksuz

M

mad *(crazy)* lud
mad *(angry)* ljut
madam(e) gospođa
magazine časopis
maid sobarica
maiden name djevojačko ime
mail pošta
mail box poštanski sanduk
main glavni
main road glavna cesta
main street glavna ulica
make, to činiti
make-up šminka
man čovjek
manager upravitelj, direktor
management uprava, rukovodstvo
manicure menikiranje
many mnogo
many a mnogi
map zemljovid
marble mramor
March ožujak
mark oznaka
market tržnica
marmalade marmelada
married *(man)* oženjen
married *(woman)* udata
marry, to vjenčati
mascara maskara
masculine muško
mask maska

mast jarbol
masterpiece remek-djelo
match žigica
material tkanina
matter tvar
as a matter of fact zapravo
it doesn't matter nije važno
what's the matter? što je?
mattress madrac
air mattress zračni madrac
maximum maksimum
May svibanj
maybe možda
mayonnaise majoneza
me ja
meal obrok
means sredstvo
mean, to značiti
meantime, in the u međuvremenu
measles ospice
measure, to mjeriti
meat meso
meat broth juha od mesa
mechanic mehaničar
medicine lijek, medicina
medieval srednjovjekovni
Mediterranean mediteranski
medium srednji
medium-rare srednje pečeno
meet, to upoznati
meeting sastanak
melon dinja
member član
men ljudi
mend popraviti
men's room muški zahod
mention, to spomenuti
menu jelovnik
merry veseo
message poruka
metal metal
meter metar
metropolis metropol
midday podne

middle sredina
Middle Ages srednji vijek
middleman posrednik
midnight ponoć
mighty moćan
migraine migrena
mild blag
mile milja
military vojni
milk mlijeko
mine moj
mineral water mineralna voda,
  kisela voda
minimum najmanji
mint metvica
minute minuta
mirror zrcalo
misfortune nesreća
miss gospođica
miss, to promašiti
  I miss you nedostaješ mi
  I missed the train zakasnio sam
  na vlak
mistake greška
Mister gospodin
misunderstanding nesporazum
mixture mješavina
mix up zabuna
modern suvremen
modern art suvremena umjetnost
modern times sadašnja vremena
moisturizer hidrantna krema
moment trenutak
monastery samostan
Monday ponedjeljak
money novac
monkey majmun
month mjesec
monument spomenik
mood raspoloženje
moon mjesec
moorings sidrište
moped moped
more više

more than više nego
  some more još malo
morning jutro
  in the morning ujutro
  this morning jutros
Moslem Musliman, muslimanski
mosque džamija
mosquito komarac
mostly najviše
mother majka
mother-in-law svekrva
motion pokret
motor motor
motorboat motorni čamac
motorcycle motocikl
mountain planina
mouse miš
moustache brkovi
mouth usta
mouth wash voda za usta
move, to (po)maknuti
move, to *(change residence)* preseliti
movies filmovi
  let's go to the movies
    hajdemo u kino
Mr. gospodin
Mrs. gospođa
much puno
  as much as onoliko koliko
  how much koliko
muffler prigušivač
muggy sparno
mule mula
multipy, to množiti
mumps zaušnjaci
municipal općinski
muscle mišić
museum muzej
music glazba
musician glazbenik
mussels dagnje
must morati
mustard senf
mutual zajednički

my moj
myself sam

N

nail nokat
  nail clippers noktorezac
  nail file turpija za nokte
  nail polish lak za nokte
  nail polish remover aceton
  nail scissors škarice za nokte
naked gol
name ime
nap, to take a prileći
napkin ubrus
narrow uzak
nasty ružan
nation država
national narodni
nationality narodnost
native country domovina
natural prirodan
naturally naravno
nature priroda
nausea mučnina
near blizu
nearly skoro
nearness blizina
neat uredan
necessary potreban
neck vrat
necklace ogrlica
necktie kravata
need, to trebati
needle igla
negate, to negirati
negative negativan
neighbor susjed
neighborhood susjedstvo
neither...nor ni...ni
nephew nečak
nerve živac
nervous živčan
net mreža
nettle kopriva

neurotic neurotičan
neutral neutralan
never nikada
new nov
news vijesti
newspaper novine
newsstand kiosk za prodaju novina
new year nova godina
New Zealand Novi Zeland
next idući
next to pokraj
next door susjedna
next of kin najbliži rod
nice simpatičan
nickname nadimak
niece nečakinja
night noć
night club noćni klub
night table noćni stol
nightmare loš san
no ne
nobody nitko
no one nitko
nod, to kimnuti
noise buka
noisy bučan
non-alcoholic bezalkoholan
none nijedan
nonsense besmislica
non-smoking za nepušače
non-stop non-stop
noodles rezanci
noon podne
normal normalan
north sjever
Norway Norveška
nose nos
not ne
note poruka
note *(money)* novčanica
notebook bilježnica
nothing ništa
notice, to opaziti
notify, to obavijestiti

November studeni
now sada
nowhere nigdje
nudist nudist
nudist beach nudistička plaža
nuisance smetnja
numb ukočen
  my leg is numb utrnula mi noga
number broj
nurse bolničarka
nursery school dječji vrtić
nuts orasi

O

oar veslo
oatmeal zobeno brašno
obligatory obavezan
obnoxious odvratan
obvious očigledan
occasionally povremeno
occupy, to zauzeti
occur, to desiti se
October listopad
octopus hobotnica
odd čudan
of od
offend, to uvrijediti
offer, to nuditi
office ured
office building poslovna zgrada
officer redarstvenik
official službeni
off season mrtva sezona
often često
oil ulje
oil pressure pritisak ulja
ointment mast
okay u redu
old star
old-fashioned staromodan
olive maslina
olive oil maslinovo ulje
omelet omlet
on na

once jedanput
once upon a time jednom
again opet
one jedan
one and a half jedan i pol
onion luk
only samo
open otvoren
open from...to... otvoreno od...do...
open, to otvoriti
opera opera
operation operacija
opportunity prilika
opposite suprotan
oppressive koji tlači
optician optičar
optimistic optimistički
optional neobavezan
or ili
orange naranča
orange juice sok od naranča
orchestra orkestar
order narudžba
order to, to naručiti
ordinary običan
organization organizacija
organize, to organizirati
original originalan
ornament ukras
other drugi
otherwise inače
ought to trebalo bi
our naš
ours naše
out van
outside vani
  outside of izvan
outlet *(electric)* utičnica
oven pećnica
over preko
over there tamo
overcharge, to previše naplatiti
overcoat ogrtač
overcooked prekuhan

overexposed preosvjetljen
overheat, to pregrijati
overnight preko noći
overpowering prejako
overweight pretežak
owe, to dugovati
own, to posjedovati
owner vlasnik
oyster kamenica

P

pace tempo
pack kutija
pack, to pakovati
pack it in, to natrpati
package paket
packet paket
paddle veslo
padlock lokot
page list
pain bol
paint, to slikati
painter slikar
painting slika
pair par
pajamas pidžama
palace palača
pale blijed
palm tree palma
palpitations palpitacije
pancake palačinka
panic panika
panties gačice
pants hlače
panty hose hulahopke
paper papir
parallel paralelan
parcel paket
pardon me oprostite
parents roditelji
park park
parking lot parkiralište
part dio
participate, to sudjelovati

partly djelomično
partner sudionik, partner
party zabava
pass, to proći
passageway prolaz
passenger putnik
passing, in u prolazu
passport putovnica
paste, to lijepiti
past prošlost
pastry kolač
pate pašteta
path put, staza
patient strpljiv
patient *(medical)* pacijent
patio teresa
pattern kroj, mustra
pavement pločnik
pay, to platiti
pay duty, to platiti carinu
pay phone govornica
paymaster blagajnik
peace and quiet mir i tišina
peach breskva
peanuts kikiriki
pear kruška
pearl perla
peas grašak
peculiar čudan
pedal pedal
pedestrian pješak
pedestrian crossing pješački prijelaz
pen penkala
pencil olovka
penetrate probiti
penicillin penicilin
penknife džepni nož
pensioner penzioner
people ljudi
pepper papar
per cent postotak
perfect savršen
perform, to nastupiti
performance nastup

perfume parfem
perhaps možda
period (of time) razdoblje
permanent wave trajna
permission odobrenje
permit propusnica
permitted, to be biti dopušteno
perpetual neprekidan
person osoba
personal osobni
perspire, to znojiti se
petrol (gasoline) benzin
pharmacy ljekarna
phone see telephone
photograph fotografija
photographer fotograf
phrase izraz
phrasebook zbirka izraza
physician liječnik
piano klavir
pick, to izabrati
pick up, to pokupiti
pickpocket džeparoš
picnic piknik
picture slika
pie pita
piece komad
pig prase
pigeon golub
pill pilula
pillow jastuk
pillowcase jastučnica
pin pribadača
pinch, to štipati
pineapple ananas
pineapple juice sok od ananas
pink ružičasta boja
pipe (smoking) lula
pipe (water) cijev
pitcher bukara
pity, it's a šteta
pizza pizza
place mjesto
place of birth mjesto rođenja

place, to staviti
plague kuga
plain jednostavan
perish, to ginuti
plan, to planirati
plane zrakoplov
plaster cast gips
plastic plastika
plastic bag najlon vrečica
plate tanjur
platform (train) peron
play, to igrati se
playground igralište
pleasant, ugodan
please molim
pleased, to be biti drago (nekome)
pleasure užitak
pliers kliješta
plug (electric) utikač
plum šljiva
plumber vodoinstalater
pneumonia upala pluća
pocket džep
pocket watch džepni sat
poet pjesnik
point šiljak
point, to pokazati prstom
poisonous otrovan
Poland Poljska
police redarstvo, policija
policeman redarstvenik, policajac
police station redarstvena ispostava
polish, to polirati
polite uljudan
polluted okužen
pond jezero
poor siromašan
pope papa
popular popularan
population pučanstvo
porcelain porculan
pork svinjetina
port luka
porter portir

Portugal Portugal
posh otmjen
possession imanje
possibility mogućnost
possible moguć
  if possible ako je moguće
post card razglednica
post office pošta
potato krumpir
  boiled potatoes kuhani krumpir
  fried potatoes pečeni krumpiri
  mashed potatoes krumpir pire
  potato chips čips
  potato salad krumpir salata
pottery keramika
pound funta
pour, to ljevati
powder puder
powdered milk mlijeko u prahu
power snaga
powerful snažan
practice, to vježbati
praise, to pohvaliti
prawns račići
pray, to moliti se
prefer, to davati prednost
pregnant u drugom stanju
premonition predosjećaj
preparation priprema
prepare, to pripremiti
prepared spreman
prescription recept
present *(gift)* poklon
present sadašnjost
  for the present za sada
preserve, to očuvati
press, to *(iron)* glačati
press, to pritisnuti
pretty lijep
prevail, to prevladati
price cijena
  raise the price povisiti cijenu
priest svećenik
print, to tiskati

printed matter tiskanice
priority prvenstvo
prison zatvor
private privatan
prize nagrada
probably vjerojatno
problem problem
proceed, to proslijediti
product proizvod
program program
promise obećanje
proper pravilan
properly kako treba
prostitute prostitutka
protect, to štititi
Protestant protestant
proud ponosan
proverb poslovica
proverbial poslovičan
prune suha šljiva
public javno
pudding puding
pull, to vući
pump pumpa
pump, to pumpati
punctual točan
puncture, to probušiti
punctured probušen
pupil učenik
pupil *(eye)* zjenica
pure čist
purple ljubičast
purse torba
push, to gurati
put, to staviti
put on, to obući
put soles on, to staviti đonove

Q

quality kvaliteta
quarantine karantena
quarter četvrt
quay kej
question pitanje

quick brz
quickly brzo
quiet tih, miran
quince dunja
quit, to prestati
quite prilično

R

rabbi rabin
rabbit kunić
rabies bjesnoća
race trka
race *(people)* rasa
racket reket
radiator *(auto)* hladnjak
rag krpa
railroad željeznica
railroad crossing željeznički prijelaz
rain kiša
rain, to padati kiša
raincoat kišna kabanica
raise, to povisiti
rape silovanje
rape, to silovati
rare rijedak
rash osip
raspberry malina
rat štakor
rate of exchange devizni tečaj
rather *(instead)* radije
rather *(quite)* prilično
raw prijesan
razor aparat za brijanje
razor blade žilet
reach, to dokučiti
  within easy reach na dohvatu
read, to čitati
ready gotov
real stvaran
reality stvarnost
realize, to ostvariti
really stvarno
rear, in the pozadi
rearview mirror retrovizor

reasonable umjeren
rebuild, to ponovo izgraditi
rebuilding izgrađivanje
receipt priznanica
receive, to primiti
recently nedavno
reception prijem
reception desk *(hotel)* recepcija
recipe recept
recognize, to prepoznati
recommend, to preporučiti
recommendation preporuka
record ploča
record player gramofon
recreation rekreacija
red crven
red wine crno vino
reduction sniženje
refer to, to uputiti na
refreshing osvježavajući
refrigerator hladnjak
refund, to vratiti novac
region područje
register, to registrirati
registered registriran
  by registered mail preporučeno
rejoice, to razveseliti
relative rođak
relatives rodbina
relax, to opustiti se
reliable pouzdan
religion vjera
remain, to ostati
remainder ostatak
remarkable izvanredan
remember, to sjećati se
remind one, to podsjetiti (koga)
remote udaljen
rent, to iznajmiti
repair, to popraviti
repairs popravci
repeat, to ponoviti
report, to izvijestiti
representative predstavnik

reputation ugled
request molba
rescue, to spasiti
reservation rezervacija
reserve, to rezervirati
reside, to stanovati
respectfully s poštovanjem
rest odmor
rest, to odmarati se
restaurant restoran
restless nemiran
retire, to umirovati se
retired umirovljen
return povratak
return, to povratiti
revenue officer carinik
reverse gear brzina za vožnju unazad
revolting odvratan
rheumatism reuma
rib rebro
ribbon vrpca
rice riža
rich bogat
ride, to voziti se
ride around, to voziti okolo
ridiculous besmislen
right desno
right away odmah
ring prsten
ring, to zvoniti
rip, to poderati
ripe zreo
rise, to dizati
risk, to riskirati
risky riskantan
river rijeka
road cesta
road map putna karta
road sign natpis
roaring bučan
roast beef pečena govedina
rob, to pokrasti
robe kućni ogrtač
robust snažan

rock kamen
roll zemička
Rome Rim
roof krov
room soba
   single room jednokrevetna soba
   double room dvokrevetna soba
   triple room trokrevetna soba
room service posluga u sobi
root korijen
rope konop
rose ruža
rough *(sea)* uzburkan
rough grubo
round okrugao
route put
rowboat čamac na vesla
rubber guma
rubber band gumica
rubbish smeće
rude neuljudan
rug tepih
ruins ruševine
rum rum
run, to trčati
   run around, to trčati okolo
rupture, to lomiti
rush, to jurnuti, srljati
Russia Rusija
Russian Rus, ruski
rye bread raženi kruh

S

saccharine saharin
sad tužan
saddle sedlo
safe siguran
safe *(noun)* sef
safety pin ziherica
sail jedro
sailboat jedrilica
sailor mornar
salad salata
sale prodaja

salt sol
salty slano
same isti
sand pijesak
sandals sandale
sandwich sendvič
sandy pjeskovit
sanitary napkin higijenski uložak
sardines sardine
satisfactory zadovoljavajuće
satisfied zadovoljan
satisfy, to zadovoljiti
Saturday subota
sauce umak
saucer tanjurić
sauna sauna
sausage kobasica
save, to spasiti
save for, to štediti za
say, to reći
   how do you say...? kako se kaže?
   what did you say? što ste rekli?
scarf marama
scent miris
schedule raspored
school škola
science znanost
scissors škare
scold, to izgrditi
score (sports) rezultat
scotch tape celotejp
scream, to vrisnuti
scruffy otrcan
scuba diving ronjenje
sea more
   by the sea kraj mora
   by sea morem
sea air morski zrak
sea urchin morski jež
seafood restaurant riblji restoran
seafront morska obala
seagull galeb
seam šav
seaport luka

search, to tražiti
seasick, to be imati morsku bolest
seasickness morska bolest
season sezona
seasoning začin
seat sjedište
seatbelt sigurnosni pojas
seaweed morska trava
secluded osamljen
second (adj.) drugi
second (time) sekunda
   just a second! samo trenutak!
second class drugi razred
second-hand polovan
secret (noun) tajna
sedative sedativ
see, to vidjeti
see again, to vidjeti ponovo
seek, to tražiti
seem, to izgledati
seemingly tobože
seldom rijetko
self-service samoposluga
self-portrait autoportret
sell, to prodavati
send, to poslati
send regards, to pozdraviti
senior citizen penzioner
sensational senzacionalan
sense, to osjećati
sensible razuman
sensitive osjećajan
sentimental sentimentalan
separate odvojen
separate, to odvajati
September rujan
Serbia Srbija
Serbian sprski
serious ozbiljan
serve, to poslužiti
service posluga
settle, to (a debt) podmiriti (dug)
several nekoliko
several times nekoliko puta

sew, to šivati
sex seks
sex *(gender)* spol
shade hlad
shady sjenovit
shake hands, to rukovati se
shake off, to otresti
shallow plitak
shame sramota
  what a shame! šteta!
shampoo šampon
shape oblik
share, to dijeliti
shark morski pas
sharp oštar
shave, to brijati
shaver aparat za brijanje
shaving brush četkica za brijanje
shaving foam pjena za brijanje
shaving soap sapun za brijanje
shawl šal
she ona
sheep ovca
sheet plahta
sheet *(paper)* list
shelf polica
shell školjka
shelter sklonište
sherry šeri
ship brod
shipment pošiljka
shirt košulja
shock šok
shock, to prestrašiti
shock-absorber amortizer
shocking šokantan
shoe cipela
shoelace vezica za cipele, žnjirač
shoemaker postolar
shop trgovina
shop window izlog
shore obala
short kratak
short *(person)* nizak

short circuit kratki spoj
shortcut prečac
shorthand stenografija
shorts kratke hlače
should trebao bi
shoulder rame
shoulder blade lopatica
shout, to vikati
show, to pokazati
shower tuš
shrimp račići
shrine hram, svetište
shrink, to skupiti se
shuffle (cards), to miješati karte
shut, to zatvoriti
shut up, to zavezati
  shut up! zaveži!
shutter *(photography)* blenda
shy povučen
sick bolestan
side strana
sidewalk pločnik
sights znamenitosti
sightseeing razgledavanje
sign natpis
sign, to potpisati
signal znak
signature potpis
significant značajan
silence tišina
silk svila
silver srebro
silverware jedaći pribor
similar sličan
simple jednostavan
simplicity jednostavnost
since *(reason)* pošto
since *(time)* od kada
sincere iskren
sing, to pjevati
singer pjevač
single room jednokrevetna soba
sink sudoper
sir gospodin

sirloin goveđi bubrežnjak

sister sestra

sister-in-law šogorica

sit, to sjediti

sit down, to sjesti

situation prilika

size veličina

ski skija

ski, to skijati se

skiing skijanje

ski boots skijaške cipele

ski lift skijaška žičara

skin koža

skin-diving ronjenje

skinny mršav

skirt suknja

skull lubanja

sky nebo

sleep spavanje

sleep, to spavati

sleeper car spavaća kola

sleeping pill pilula za spavanje

sleepy pospan

sleeve rukav

slice komad, kriška

slide *(photography)* dijapozitiv

slim vitak

slip *(paper)* ceduljica

slip *(clothing)* podsuknja

slippery klizav

slow spor

slow, to be (watch) kasniti

slowly polako

small malen

small change sitniš

smart pametan

smell miris

smile smiješak

smile, to smiješiti se

smoke dim

smoke, to pušiti

smoking room soba za pušenje

smooth gladak

snack zalogaj

snake zmija

sneakers tenisice

snob snob

snorkel cijev za disanje

snow snijeg

snow, to padati snijeg

so tako, dakle

so far do sada

so that tako da

soaked mokar do kože

soap sapun

sober trijezan

soccer nogomet

sock čarapa

socket utikač

sofa kauč

soft mekan

soiled prljav

sold out rasprodano

soldier vojnik

sole đon

sole *(fish)* list

solid solidan

somebody netko

something nešto

sometime kadgod

sometimes ponekad

somewhere negdje

son sin

song pjesma

son-in-law zet

soon uskoro

   as soon as... čim...

sore, to be boljeti

sorry, I am žao mi je

sort vrsta

soul duša

soup juha

sour kiseo

south jug

South Africa Južna Afrika

South America Južna Amerika

souvenir suvenir

spa toplice

space prostor
space heater grijalica
Spain Španjolska
Spaniard Španjolac
spanish španjolski
spare part rezervni dio
spare tire rezervna guma
spark plug svjećica
speak, to govoriti
special poseban
specialty specijalitet
spectator gledatelj
speed brzina
speed limit ograničenje brzine
speedboat gliser
speedometer brzinomjer
spell, to pisati
spend, to trošiti
spice mirodija
spice, to začiniti
spider pauk
spill, to prosuti
spinach špinat
spirit duh
spite of, in usprkos
splendid divan
splinter iver
sponge spužva
spoon žlica
sport šport
spot mrlja
sprain, to uganuti
spring, feder
spring *(season)* proljeće
square *(city)* trg
stain mrlja
staircase stubište
stairs stube
stale star
stamp marka
stand, to stajati
standard standardan
star zvijezda
start početak

start, to početi
start, to *(auto)* okrenuti
starter pokretač
starve, to biti gladan
state *(condition)* stanje
state *(country)* država
stateroom luksuzna kabina
station postaja
station *(bus)* autobusni kolodvor
station *(railroad)* željeznički kolodvor
statue kip
stay, to ostati
steak biftek
steal, to ukrasti
steamer parobrod
steep strm
steering wheel upravljač
stenographer stenograf(kinja)
step korak
step, to koracati
stereo stereo
sterling sterling
stew pirjano jelo
steward stjuard
stewardess stjuardesa
sticky ljepljivo
stiff ukočen
still *(quiet)* mirno
   I am still waiting. Još čekam.
stimulate, to poticati, stimulirati
stimulation poticanje
sting ubosti
stink smrditi
stocking čarapa
stolen ukrađen
stomach želudac
stomachache bol u želucu
stone kamen
stop, to stati
store trgovina
storm oluja
story priča
stove štednjak
straight ravan

straight ahead ravno naprijed
strange čudan
stranger neznanac
strap remen
strawberry jagoda
stream potok
street ulica
streetcar tramvaj
street map plan grada
strength snaga
strenuous naporno
strep throat upala grla
stretch, to rastegnuti
strike, to udariti
string špaga
striped prugast
strive for, to težiti za
stroll, to prošetati se
stroller kolica za bebu
strong jak, snažan
struggle borba
stuck zaglavljen
student student
study, to učiti
stupid glup
sty ječmenac
style stil
substantial priličan
subtract, to oduzimati
suburb predgrađe
successful uspješan
such takav
suddenly iznenadno
sue, to tužiti
suede antilop koža
suffering patnja
sugar šećer
suggest predlagati
suit odijelo
suit, to odgovarati
suitable odgovarajuće
suitcase kovčeg
sum suma, svota
summer ljeto

sun sunce
sunbathe sunčati se
sunburn opeklina od sunca
Sunday nedjelja
sunglasses sunčane naočale
sunny sunčano
sunrise izlazak sunca
sunset zalazak sunca
suntan lotion losion za sunčanje
super super
supper večera
supplement *(monetary)* doplata
sure sigurno
surname prezime
surprise iznenađenje
surprise, to iznenaditi
suspension *(auto)* opruge točkova
surround, to opkoliti
suspicious sumnjiv
swallow, to (pro)gutati
swearword psovka
sweat, to znojiti se
sweater vesta, džemper
sweatshirt majica
Swede Šveđanin, Šveđanka
Sweden Švedska
Swedish švedski
sweet sladak
sweeten, to posladiti
sweets slatkiši
swell, to naticati
swim, to plivati
swimming plivanje
swimming pool bazen
Swiss švicarski
switch, to zamijeniti
switch on, to upaliti
switch off, to ugasiti
Switzerland Švicarska
swollen nateknut
sympathy suosjećajnost
synagogue sinagoga
synthetic sintetičan

T

table stol
table tennis stolni tenis
table wine stolno vino
tablecloth stolnjak
tablespoon velika žlica
tactfully na fin način
tailor krojač
tail light stražje svijetlo
take, to uzeti
take care of, to čuvati
take a rest, to odmarati se
take off, to skinuti
take out, to izvaditi
take over, to preuzeti
take place, to dogoditi se
talcum powder talk
talk, to govoriti
tall visok
tampons tamponi
tan, to pocrniti
tape vrpca
tape measure krojački centimetar
tape recorder magnetofon
taste ukus
taste, to okusiti
taste good, to biti ukusno
tax-free oslobođen od poreza
taxi taksi
taxi driver taksista
taxi stand taksi stajalište
tea čaj
teach, to učiti
teacher učitelj(ica)
team momčad
teapot čajnik
tear suza
tear, to poderati
tear open, to rastrgati
tease, to tentati
teaspoon žličica
technical stručno
telegram telegram, brzojav

telephone telefon, brzoglas
telephone book telefonski imenik
telephone number telefonski broj
telephone, to telefonirati, nazvati
telephoto lens teleobjektiv
television televizor
tell, to reći, kazati
temperature temperatura
temple hram
temporary privremen
tempting zamamno
tenant stanar
tennis tenis
tennis court tenis igralište
tent šator
term rok
terminal station krajnja postaja
terrace terasa
terrible strašan
terrific silan
than nego
thank, to zahvaliti
thanks, thank you hvala
that to
that is that much to je toliko
that one onaj, taj
the taj, ta, to
theater kazalište
their njihov
theirs njihovo
them
  for them za njih
  to them njima
  with them s njima
  from them od njih
then onda
there tamo
therefore zato, zbog toga
thermal springs toplice
thermometer termometar
thermos termos
thermostat termostat
these ovi
they oni

thick debeo
thief lopov
thigh bedro
thin tanak
thing stvar
think, to misliti
third treći
third, a trećina
third class treći razred
this ovaj, ova, ovo
those oni
thread konac
three tri
three times tri puta
throat grlo
through kroz
throw, to baciti
throw up, to povratiti
thumb palac
thunder grmljavina
thunderstorm oluja s grmljavinom
Thursday četvrtak
ticket ulaznica
ticket window blagajna
tie kravata
tiger tigar
tight tjesan
tighten, to stisnuti
till do
time vrijeme
  at that time u to vrijeme
  for the time being zasada
timetable raspored
tiny majušan
tip *(to waiter, etc.)* napojnica
tire guma
tired umoran
tissues papirnate maramice
to do
toast *(bread)* kruh prepečenac
toast *(drink)* zdravica
tobacco duhan
today danas
today's današnji

toe nožni prst
together zajedno
toilet zahod
toilet paper toaletni papir
toll cestarina
tomato rajčica
tomato juice sok od rajčica
tomato sauce umak od rajčica
tomorrow sutra
  day after tomorrow preksutra
ton tona
tongue jezik
tonic tonik
tonight večeras
tonsils krajnici
too također
tooth zub
toothache zubobolja
toothbrush četkica za zube
toothpaste pasta za zube
total sveukupno
touch, to dirati
touching dodirujuće
tough žilav
tour putovanje
tour guide vodič
tourist turista
tourist trade turizam
tow, to šlepati
toward prema
towel ručnik
town gradić
town hall gradska vijećnica
tower toranj
toy igračka
trace trag
track suit trenirka
traffic promet
traffic light semafor
trailer prikolica
train vlak
  express train brzi vlak
train station željeznički kolodvor
tranquilizers umirujuća sredstva

transcribe, to prepisati
transformer transformator
translate, to prevoditi
translator prevoditelj(ica)
translation prijevod
transmission *(auto)* tranzmisija
travel, to putovati
travel agency putnička agencija
travelers' check putnički ček
traveling bag putnička torba
traveling companion suputnik
tray tacna
tree drvo
tremendous silan
tricky kompliciran
trip putovanje
tripod tronožac
tropical tropski
trouble nezgoda
trousers hlače
trout pastrva
truck kamion
truck driver vozač kamiona
true istinit
  that's not true to nije istina
truly yours Vaš odani
t-shirt majica
trump adut
trunk *(auto)* prtljažnik
try, to pokušati
try out, to isprobati
Tuesday utorak
tuna fish tunina
tune melodija
tunnel tunel
Turk Turčin, Turkinja
Turkey Turska
turkey *(meat)* puretina
Turkish turski
turn *(road)* zavoj
turn, to skrenuti
turn off, to isključiti
turn on, to upaliti
turning skretanje

TV televizija
tweezers pinceta
twice dvaput
tow, to šlepati
twins blizanci
twist, to uganuti
two dva
two and a half dva i pol
type vrsta
type, to tipkati
typewriter pisaći stroj
typhoid tifus
typical tipičan

U

ugly ružan
ulcer čir
umbrella kišobran
uncle ujak, tetak, stric
uncomfortable neudoban
unconscious nesvjestan
under ispod
underground podzemni
underpants gaće
undershirt podkošulja
understand, to razumijeti
understanding razumijevanje
undertake, to poduzeti
underwear donje rublje
undo otkopčati
unemployed nezaposlen
uneven neravan
unfair nepravedan
unfinished nesvršen
unforgettable nezaboravan
unfortunately na žalost
unfriendly neprijazan
unhappy nesretan
unhealthy nezdrav
unique jedinstven
unit jedinica
unite, to ujediniti
United States of America
  Sjedinjene Američke Države

university sveučilište
unlimited neograničen
unlimited mileage
  neograničena kilometraža
unlock, to otključati
unmarried *(man)* neoženjen
unmarried *(woman)* neudata
unpack, to otpakovati
unpleasant neugodan
unpronounceable
  koji se ne može izgovoriti
untie, to odvezati
until do, dok (ne)
unusual neobičan
unwillingly nesklon
up gore
up to now sve do sada
upon na
upset stomach pokvaren želudac
upside down naopako
upstairs gore
upstairs, to go ići gore
upward prema gore
urgent hitan
urinary tract infection
  infekcija mokraćnih organa
us nas
  with us s nama
  for us za nas
use uporaba
use, to koristiti
useful koristan
usual običan
usually obično

vacancy slobodnih soba
vacation odmor
vaccination cijepljenje
vacuum cleaner usisavač
valid važeći
valley dolina
valuable dragocjen
value vrijednost

van kombi
vanilla vanilija
vase vaza
veal teletina
vegetables povrće
vegetarian vegeterijanac
velvet samt
vending machine automat
ventilator ventilator
very veoma
vest prsluk
via preko
vicinity blizina
victim žrtva
video video
view pogled
vigorous energičan
villa vila
village selo
vine loza
vinegar ocat
vineyard vinograd
visa viza
visit posjet
visit, to posjetiti
vital bitan
vitamins vitamini
vodka votka
voice glas
voltage voltaža
vomit, to povraćati
vow zakletva
vow, to zavjetovati se
voyage putovanje

waist struk
wait, to čekati
waiter konobar
waiting čekanje
waiting room čekaonica
waitress konobarica
wake up, to probuditi
walk, to hodati

walk, to go for a šetati se
walking šetanje
wall zid
wallet novčarka
walnut orah
wander, to lutati
waltz valcer
want, to htjeti
war rat
  world war svijetski rat
ward odjel
wardrobe garderoba
warm topao
warning upozorenje
wash, to prati
washcloth krpica za lice
wash basin umivaonik
washing machine
  stroj za pranje rublja
wasp osa
wasteful rastrošan
wastepaper basket koš za smeće
watch, to gledati
watch ručni sat
watchmaker urar
water voda
water skiing skijanje na vodi
waterproof nepromočiv
wave val
wave, to mahati
way *(method)* način
way *(direction)* put
we mi
weak slab
wealth bogatstvo
wealthy bogat
wear, to nositi
wear out, to istrošiti
weather vrijeme
wedding vjenčanje
Wednesday srijeda
week tjedan
weekend vikend
weight težina

weird čudan
welcome dobrodošlica
welcome, you are molim
well bunar, zdenac
well dobar
  as well as kao i
west zapad
wet mokar
what što
  of what od čega
wheel kotač
wheelchair invalidska kolica
when kada
where gdje
  to where kamo, kuda
whereupon našto
whether or ili...ili
whether or not da ili ne
which koji
while dok
  awhile neko vrijeme
whipped cream šlag, tučeno vrhnje
whiskey viski
whisper, to šaptati
white bijel
who tko
whoever tko bilo
whole potpun
whooping cough hripavac
whose čiji
why zašto
wide širok
widow udovica
widower udovac
wife supruga, žena
wig perika
will volja
win, to pobijediti
wind vjetar
wind, to *(a watch)* naviti
winding vijugav
window prozor
window seat sjedište pored prozora
windy vjetrovit

wine vino
wine list vinska karta
wing krilo
winter zima
winter holiday zimski odmor, zimovanje
wire žica
wisdom mudrost
wish, želja
wish, to željeti
with sa
within iznutra
without bez
witness svjedok
witty duhovit
woman žena
wonder, to čuditi se
wonderful divan
wood drvo
woods šuma
wool vuna
word riječ
work posao
work, to raditi
work of art umjetničko djelo
works djela
world svijet
worn down istrošen
worry, to brinuti se
worse gore
worse, to get pogoršati se
worst najgori
worth vrijednost
wrap, to umotati
wrapping omot
wrapping paper omotni papir
wrench ključ za odvijanje
wrist ručni zglob
wrist watch ručni sat
write, to pisati

write down, to napisati
writer pisac
writing pisanje
writing paper papir za pisanje
wrong krivo
  to be wrong ne biti u pravo

X-ray rendgenske zrake
xerox, to fotokopirati
xeroxing fotokopiranje

yacht jahta
yard dvorište
year godina
yellow žut
yes da
yesterday jučer
  day before yesterday prekjučer
yet već
  has it arrived yet? je li već stiglo?
  it has not arrived yet nije još stiglo
yoghurt jogurt
you Vi (polite), ti (familiar)
young mlad
your Vaš, tvoj
yours Vaše, tvoje
youth *(period of life)* mladost
youth *(person)* mladić
youth hostel omladinski hotel
your health, to! živio!

Z

zero ništica
zip code poštanski broj
zipper patentni zatvarač
zoo zoološki vrt
zoom lens zum-objektiv
zucchini bučice

CROATIAN-ENGLISH
DICTIONARY

A

aceton nail polish remover
adresar address book
adut trump
aerodrom airport
agencija agency
ako if
aktovka briefcase
aktualan current
alat tools
alergičan allergic
alergija allergy
ali but
alkohol alcohol
alkoholičar alcoholic
alkoholno piće liquor, booze
Alpe Alps
alternativa alternative
alternator alternator
ambasada embassy
ambasador ambassador
američki American
Amerika America
Amerikanac, Amerikanka American
amortizer shock-absorber
ananas pineapple
anđeo angel
angina angina
animirani film animated film
antagonizam antagonism
antibiotik antibiotic
antikni antique
antikvarijat antique shop
antilop koža suede
aparat apparatus
aperitiv aperitif
apsces abscess
apsolutno absolutely
arheologija archeology
arhitekt architect
arhitektura architecture
aspirin aspirin
Atlantik Atlantic

atmosfera atmosphere
Australija Australia
Australijanac Australian
australski Australian
Austria Austria
Austrijanac, Austrijanka Austrian
austrijski Austrian
auto-servis auto repair shop
auto automobile
autobus bus
autobusna postaja bus stop
autobusni kolodvor bus station
automat vending machine
automatski automatic
autoportret self-portrait
autoput highway
autostoper hitchhiker
avenija avenue
avion airplane

B

baciti to throw
baka grandmother
bakalar cod
balkon balcony
banka bank
banket banquet
bankovni račun bank account
barbun red mullet
barem at least
barjak flag
barmen bartender
barokni Baroque
baš tako just so
baš sada just now
baterija flashlight, battery
bazen swimming pool
beba baby
bečki odrezak Wiener Schnitzel
bedro thigh
benzin gasoline
benzinska postaja gas station
benzinski rezervoar gas tank
besmislen ridiculous

besmislica nonsense
bez without
bezalkoholan non-alcoholic
bezbrižan carefree, happy-go-lucky
bezplatan free of charge
bež beige
bicikl bicycle
bife buffet
biftek steak
bijel white
bijela kava coffee with milk
bijeli luk garlic
bilijar billiards
bilježnica notebook
biljke herbs
bitan vital
biti to be
bitno essential
bjelilo bleach
bjesnoća rabies
bježati to flee
blag mild
blagajna cashier, ticket window
blagajnik cashier, teller
blagdan holiday
blagoslov blessing
blagovaonica dining room
blenda shutter *(photography)*
blic flash *(camera)*
blijed pale
blizanci twins
blizina proximity, vicinity
blizu close, near
blokiran blocked
blomba filling *(tooth)*
blombirati to fill *(a tooth)*
bluza blouse
boca bottle
Bog God
bogat rich, wealthy
bogatstvo wealth
boja color
bojati to dye
bojati se to be frightened

bok uz bok side by side
bokal pitcher
bol ache, pain
bol u leđima backache
bolest disease, illness
bolestan sick, ill
boljeti to hurt
bolji better
bolnica hospital
bolničarka nurse
bomba bomb
bombon candy
borba struggle
bordo burgundy
boriti se to fight
borovnice black currants
Bosanac, Bosanka Bosnian
bosanski lonac Bosnian casserole
Bosna Bosnia
božanski divine
Božić Christmas
brada chin, beard
branik fender
brašno flour
brat brother
brava lock
brdo hill
brdovit hilly
breskva peach
brijač barber
brijačnica barber shop
brijati to shave
brinuti se to worry
Britanija Britain
brkovi moustache
brod boat, ship
Brodet Dalmatian fish stew
broj number
brojiti to count
brojka figure *(number)*
broš brooch
brošura brochure
brtvilo gasket
brz fast, quick

brzi vlak fast train
brzina speed, gear
brzinomjer speedometer
brzo quickly
brzoglas telephone
brzojav telegram
bubreg kidney
bučan noisy
bučice zucchini
budilica alarm clock
budućnost future
Bugarska Bulgaria
buha flea
buka noise
bukara pitcher
bunar well
burgundac burgundy wine
busola compass
but(ica) leg *(of meat)*
butik boutique

C

carina customs
carinik customs officer
carstvo empire
ceduljica slip of paper
celer celery
celofan cellophane
celotejp scotch tape
celzij celsius, centigrade
centar center
centar grada city center
centimetar centimeter
cesta road
cestarina toll
cigara cigar
cigareta cigarette
cigla brick
cijeli all
cijelo entire
cijena price
cijepljenje vaccination
cijev pipe *(water)*
cijev za disanje snorkel

cikla beet
cikorija chicory
cipal grey mullet
cipela shoe
cjenovnik price list
crkva church
crn black
Crna Gora Montenegro
Crnogorac, Crnogorka Montenegrin
crnka brunette
crno vino red wine
crtani (film) cartoon
crtati to draw
crven red
Crveni Križ Red Cross
crveni luk onion
curiti to leak
cvijet flower
cvjećar florist
cvjetača cauliflower

č

čaj tea
čaj s limunom lemon tea
čajnik teapot
čak even
čamac na vesla rowboat
čamac za spasavanje lifeboat
čar charm
čarapa sock
čaroban charming (place or thing)
časopis magazine
čaša glass (drinking)
ček check
čekanje waiting
čekaonica waiting room
čekati to wait
čekić hammer
čelav bald
čelo forehead
čep cork
čest frequent
čestitam! Congratulations!

čestitati (kome) to congratulate
često often
češalj comb
češljati to comb
češnjak garlic
četiri four
četka brush
četkica za usne lip brush
četkica za zube toothbrush
četrdeset forty
četvrt quarter
   tri čevrt dva a quarter to two
četvrtak Thursday
četvrtina a fourth
čiji whose
čim as soon as...
činiti to make
činjenica fact
čips chips
čir boil *(on body)*
čir ulcer
čist pure, clean
čistiti to clean
čitati to read
čizma boot
član member
članak ankle
čok *(auto)* choke
čokolada chocolate
čovjek man
čudan odd
čudan peculiar
čudan weird
čudan strange
čuditi se to wonder
čuti to hear
čuvati to take care of
čuvaj se psa beware of dog
čuven famous
čvor knot

Ć

ćevapčići mini grilled meat rolls

D

da yes
da ili ne whether or not
dagnje mussels
dah breath
dakle therefore
Dalmacija Dalmatia
dalek far
dalje farther, further
daljina distance
Dalmatinac, Dalmatinka Dalmatian
dalmatinski Dalmatian
dame checkers
dan day
dan za danom day by day
danas today
današnji today's
danima for days
danju by day
Danska Denmark
daska board
dati poruku (kome) to give a message
dati to give
datula date *(fruit)*
datum date
datum rođenja date of birth
davati prednost to prefer
debeo fat, thick
dečko boyfriend
deka blanket
desiti se to occur
desno right *(direction)*
deterdžent detergent
devalviran devalued
devize hard currency
devizni tečaj rate of exchange
dezoderans deodorant
dijabetičar diabetic
dijalekt dialect
dijapozitiv slide *(photography)*
dijeca children
dijeliti to share
dijeta diet

dijete child
diktirati to dictate
dim smoke
dimljen smoked
dimnjak chimney
dinja melon
dio part
dići se to get up
diploma degree
dirati to touch
direktni vlak through train
direktor manager
disati to breathe
disko disco
distilirana voda distilled water
divan wonderful
diviti se to admire
divljač game
dizalica jack (auto)
dizati to rise, to lift
dizel diesel (fuel)
dječak boy
dječja stolica high chair
dječji children's
dječji vrtić nursery school
djed grandfather
djela works
djelomično partly
djetinstvo childhood
djevojačko ime maiden name
djevojka girl, young lady
dnevnik diary, journal
dno bottom
do until, to
do sad by now
do sada so far
do viđenja goobye
dob age
dobar good
dobar tek! bon appétit!
dobro well
dobro došli u... welcome to...
dobro jutro good morning
dobro pečen well-done

doći to come, to arrive
doći do to get to
dodati to add
dodatni extra
dodirujuće touching
dogoditi se to happen, to take place
dohvatu, na within easy reach
dok until, while
dok... by the time...
dokučiti to reach
dokument document
dolar dollar
dolazak arrival
dolina valley
dolje downstairs
domaći homemade
domaći letovi domestic flights
domaćica housewife
dom home
domovina homeland
donijeti to bring
donje rublje underwear
dopisivanje correspondence
dopisivati se to correspond
dopisnice postcards
doplata supplement (monetary)
doprinijeti to contribute
dopuniti to complete
dopustiti to let, to allow
dopustiti pristup to admit
dopušten permitted
dopuštena brzina speed limit
dopuštena težina weight limit
dopuštena visina maximum height
doručak breakfast
dosadan boring
dostupan available
dovoljno enough
dovršiti to finish
doza dosage
dozvoljen allowed
doživjeti to experience
drag dear
drage volje gladly

dragocjen valuable
dragulj jewel
dražba auction
drevan ancient
držati to keep, to hold
država state, country
državljanin citizen
drugi other, second
drugi razred second class
drvo wood, tree
dubina depth
dubok deep
dug long
dugme button
dugovati to owe
duh spirit, ghost
duhan tobacco
duhovit witty
dunja quince
duša soul
dužina length
dva two
dva put twice
dvorište yard

DŽ

džamija mosque
džem jam
džemper sweater
džep pocket
džeparoš pickpocket
džepni nož pocketknife
džepni sat pocket watch
džin gin
džin i tonik gin and tonic

Đ

đon sole
đonove, staviti to put soles on
đuveč meat and vegetable casserole

E

efikasan efficient

elastika elastic
elegantan elegant
električan electric
električar electrician
emocionalan emotional
energičan energetic, vigorous
energija energy
Engleska England
engleski English
Engleskinja Englishwoman
Englez Englishman
epileptičar epileptic
erotičan erotic
espresso espresso coffee
Europa Europe
europski European

F

faksikl file folder
fazan pheasant
feder spring
feferonke hot chili peppers
fen za kosu hair dryer
file fillet
film film
filtar filter
fino fine *(adj.)*
Finska Finland
flanel flannel
flaster bandaid
formalan formal
fotelja arm chair
foto aparat camera
fotograf photographer
fotografija photograph
fotokopiranje photocopying, xeroxing
Francuska France
francuski French
Francuskinja Frenchwoman
Francuz Frenchman
frizer(ka) hairdresser
frizerski salon hairdressing salon
funta pound

G

gaće underpants
gaćice panties
galeb seagull
galerija umjetnosti art gallery
garancija guarantee
garaža garage
garderoba cloakroom, baggage checkroom
gatara fortune teller
gaziran carbonated, fizzy
gdje where
generator generator
gibanica Croatian layered cheese pie
ginekolog gynecologist
ginuti to perish
gips plaster cast
girice smelts
gitara guitar
glačalo iron
glačati to iron
glad hunger
gladak smooth
gladan hungry
glas voice
glasan loud
glava head
glavni main, chief
glavni grad capital city
glavobolja headache
glazba music
glazbenik musician
gledatelj spectator
gledati to look, to watch
gliser speedboat
gljive mushrooms
globa fine *(monetary)*
gluh deaf
glumac actor
glumica actress
glup foolish, stupid
gnoj discharge
godina year

godišnje annually
gol naked
golf golf
golub dove, pigeon
gorak bitter
gore up, upstairs
gore worse
gorijeti to burn
gospođa (gđa) lady, Mrs.
gospođica (gđica) Miss
gospodin gentleman, mister, sir, Mr.
gost guest
gostionica eatery
gostoprimstvo hospitality
gotov finished, ready
gotski Gothic
govedina beef
govoriti to speak, to talk
govornica pay phone
grad city
gradić town
graditi to construct
gradska vijećnica city hall
građanin citizen
grah bean(s)
grč cramp
Grčka Greece
grčki Greek
gramatika grammar
gramofon record player
grana branch, limb
granica border
grašak peas
greška error, mistake
grep(frut) grapefruit
grijač heater
grijalica space heater
grijanje heating
gripa flu
Grk, Grkinja Greek
grlo throat
grmljavina thunder
groblje cemetary
grozan awful, gross

grozan ghastly
groznica fever
grožđe grapes
grožđice raisins
grub coarse, rough
grudi chest
grudnjak brassiere
grupa group
guma rubber, tire
gumica rubber band
guraj push
gurati to push
guska goose
gušter lizard
gutati to swallow

H

haljina dress
hauba hood (auto)
helikopter helicopter
hepatitis hepatitis
Hercegovac, Hercegovka Herzegovinian
hercegovski Herzegovinian
Hercegovina Herzegovina
higijenski uložak sanitary napkin
hitan urgent
hitni slučaj emergency
hlače pants
hlad shade
hladan cold
hladnjak refrigerator, radiator *(auto)*
hladno chilly
hljeb loaf
hobotnica octopus
hodati to walk
hodnik corridor, hall
homoseksualan homosexual
hotel hotel
hrabar brave
hram shrine, temple
hrana food
hren horseradish
hrenovka hot dog

hripavac whooping cough
Hrvat(ica) Croatian
hrvatsko Croatian
Hrvatska Croatia
htjeti to want
hulahopke panty hose
hvala thanks, thank you

I

i and
iako although
ići to go
ideja idea
idealan ideal
idući next
igla needle
igra game
igračka toy
igralište playground
igrati (se) to play
ikada ever
ikra caviar
ilegalan illegal
ili or
ili...ili either...or, whether...or...
imanje possession
imati to have
ime name
imenik (telefonski) telephone directory
imenovati to name
imigracija immigration
imigrant immigrant
imitacija imitation
imovina belongings
impresionirati to impress
imućan affluent
inače otherwise
Indija India
Indijac Indian
Indijanac American Indian
indijanski American Indian
indijski Indian
industrija industry

infarkt heart attack
inflacija inflation
informacije information
informirati to inform
injekcija injection
inozemstvo abroad
insekticid insecticide
insistirati to insist
insulin insulin
intelektualac intellectual
inteligentan intelligent
invalid disabled, invalid
Irac Irishman
Irska Ireland
irski Irish
iscrpljen exhausted
iseljenik emigrant
isključiti to turn off
iskrcati se to go ashore
iskren earnest, sincere
iskusan experienced
iskustvo experience
ispasti to fall out
ispit test
ispod below, under
isporučiti to deliver
isporuka delivery
ispred in front of
ispričati se to apologize, to excuse oneself
isprika apology, excuse
isprobati to try out
ispuhana guma flat tire
ispuniti to fulfill, to fill out
ispušna cijev exhaust *(auto)*
istarski Istrian
isteklo je it's expired
isti same
istinit true
istok east
Istra Istria
Istranin, Istranka Istrian
istraživati to investigate
istrošen worn out

istrošiti to wear out
Italija Italy
iver splinter
iverak flounder *(fish)*
iz from
iza beyond, behind
izabrati to select, elect, choose
izbjeći to avoid
izgledati to appear, to seem
izgovor excuse
izgraditi to build up
izgradivanje rebuilding
izgubiti to lose
izići to go out, to exit, come out
izlaz exit, gate
izlaz broj... gate number
izlazak sunca sunrise
izlet excursion
izliječiti to cure
izlog shop window display
izložba exhibition
između between
izmjena alteration, change
izmjeniti to exchange
iznad above
iznajmiti to let, to rent
iznenađenje surprise
iznenaditi to surprise
iznenadno suddenly
iznos amount
iznutra from within
izoliran isolated
izračunati to calculate
izraz expression, phrase
izuzetak exception
izvaditi to take out
izvan outside of
izvan grada in the country
izvanredan unusual, remarkable
izvijestiti to report
izvoz export
izvoziti to export
izvrsno! excellent!
izvrstan excellent

J

ja I, me
jabuka apple
jabukovac cider
jabukovača apple brandy
jačanje fortification
Jadransko more Adriatic Sea
jagoda strawberry
jahanje horseback riding
jahta yacht
jaje egg
jak strong
jakna jacket
janjeći but leg of lamb
janjeći odrezak lamb chop
janjetina lamb
jarak ditch
jarbol mast
jasan clear
jastog lobster
jastučnica pillowcase
jastuk pillow
javno public
je is
ječmenac sty
jedan one
jedanput once
jedaći pribor silverware
jedinica unit
jedinstven unique
jednokrevetna soba single room
jednom once upon a time
jednostavan simple, plain
jedrilica sailboat
jedro sail
jedva hardly, barely
jeftin cheap
jelo course *(of meal)*
jelovnik menu
jer because
jesen autumn
jesti to eat
jestiv edible

jetra liver
jetrena pašteta liver paté
jezero lake
jezik language, tongue
jod iodine
jogurt yoghurt
jučer yesterday
jug south
juha soup
jutro morning
jutros this morning
Južna Amerika South America
Južna Afrika South Africa

K

kabare cabaret
kabina cabin
kaciga helmet
kada when
kadgod anytime
kafić café
kajgana scrambled eggs
kajsije apricots
kakao cocoa
kako how
kalendar calendar
kalorije calories
kamate interest *(financial)*
kamen rock, stone
kamenica oyster
kamion truck
kamo (to) where
kamp camp
kampiralište campgrounds
kampiranje camping
Kanađanin, Kanađanka Canadian
Kanada Canada
kanadski Canadian
kanal channel
kanu canoe
kao as, like
kapela chapel
kapetan captain
kapi drops

kapija gate
kapital capital *(money)*
kaput coat
karakter character
karanfil carnation
karantena quarantine
karta card, ticket
karton carton
kartonska kutija cardboard box
kasarna barracks
kasino casino
kasnije later
kasniti to be late, to be delayed
kasno late
kašalj cough
katalog catalog
katastrofa disaster
katedrala cathedral
katolički Catholic
Katolik Catholic
kauč couch, sofa
kava coffee
kavana café
kazališna blagajna box office
kazalište theater
kazeta cassette
kazna fine *(monetary)*
kči daughter
kej quay
keks biscuit, cookie
kemijski chemical
kemijsko čišćenje dry cleaning
keramika ceramics, pottery
kesten chestnut
kiflice crescents (croissants)
kikiriki peanuts
kilogram kilo
kilometar kilometer
kimnuti to nod
Kina China
kineski Chinese
Kinez Chinese
kino cinema
kip statue

kipjeti to boil
kisela voda mineral water
kiseli kupus pickled cabbage
kiselo mlijeko buttermilk
kiselo vrhnje sour cream
kiselo zelje pickled cabbage
kiseo sour
kiša rain
kišna kabanica raincoat
kišobran umbrella
klasičan classical
klavir piano
kliješta pliers
klima climate
klimatizacija air conditioning
klinac kid
klinika clinic
klizav slippery
ključ key
ključ za odvijanje wrench
klub club
knjiga book
knedla dumpling
knjižara bookstore
knjižnica library
kobasica sausage
kockarnica gambling casino
kočnica brake
koji which
koktel cocktail
kola car
kola za spavanje sleeping car
kolač od jabuka apple cake
kolač od sira cheesecake
kolač pastry, cake
kolega colleague
koliko how many, how much
koljeno knee
kolosijek platform
kolovoz August
komad piece
komarac mosquito
kombi van
kombinacija combination

kombinirati to combine
komfor comfort
kompliciran complicated, tricky
kompliment compliment
kompot stewed fruit
konačno finally
konac thread, end
koncert concert
koncertna dvorana concert hall
kondenzator *(auto)* condenser
kondukter conductor
konj horse
konobar waiter
konobarica waitress, barmaid
konop rope
kontaktne leće contact lenses
kontinent continent
kontrola control
kontrolirati to control
konzerva can
konzervativan conservative
konzul consul
konzulat consulate
kopati to dig
kopča fastener, clip
kopča za kosu barrette
kopija copy
kopirati to copy
kopriva nettle
koracati to step
korak step
kord-samt corduroy
korijen root
koristan useful
koristiti to use
korizma lent
kosa hair
kost bone
košara basket
koštati to cost
košulja shirt
koš za smeće wastepaper basket
kotač wheel
kotur bicycle

kovčeg suitcase
kovani novac coins
koza goat
kozice chickenpox
kozji sir goat's cheese
kozmetičarka beautician
kozmetički salon beauty salon
kozmetika cosmetics
koža skin, leather
krafna doughnut
kraj *(n.)* end
kraj *(prep.)* by
krajnici tonsils
krajnja postaja terminal station
krajnje extremely
krajolik landscape
krasan lovely
krastavac cucumber
kratak brief, short
kratke hlače shorts
kratki spoj short circuit
krava cow
kravata necktie
kredenc dresser
kreditna kartica credit card
krema cream
krevet bed
krilo wing
kriška slice
kriv guilty
krivnja fault
krivo wrong
kriza crisis
kroj cut, pattern
krojač tailor
krojački centimetar tape measure
krov roof
kroz through
krpa rag
krstarenje cruise
krug circle
kruh bread
krumpir potato
krumpir pire mashed potatoes

krumpir pita potato pie
kruna crown
kruška pear
kruškovača pear brandy
krv blood
krvariti to bleed
krvav bloody, rare
krvavica blood sausage
krznar furrier
krzno furs
kucajte prije ulaska knock before entering
kucati to knock
kuća house
kućni ogrtač robe
kuda to where
kuga plague
kuglana bowling alley
kuglanje bowling
kuhan cooked, boiled
kuhar chef
kuhar(ica) cook
kuharstvo cuisine
kuhati to cook
kuhinja kitchen
kuk hip
kukac insect, bug
kukuruz corn
kukuruzni kruh cornbread
kula castle
kultura culture
kulturan cultural
kum godfather
kuma godmother
kumče godchild
kunić rabbit
kupaće gaće bathing trunks
kupaći kostim bathing suit
kupaonica bathroom
kupe train compartment
kupiti to buy
kupus cabbage
kušet couchette
kutija box, carton, pack

kutija cigareta carton of cigarettes
kvačilo clutch
kvaliteta quality

L

labav loose
ladica drawer
lagati to lie
lakat elbow
lako easy
lakom greedy
lakomost greed
lampa lamp
lanac chain
lav lion
lažan false
led ice
leđa back *(body part)*
legalan legal
legitimacija identification papers
lekcija lesson
leća lens (contact)
leptir butterfly
let flight *(airplane)*
letjeti to fly
ležaj berth, bunk
ležaljka deck-chair
ležati to lie (down)
lice face
licitacija auction
lift elevator
lignje squid
liječnik doctor
lijek medicine, medication
lijen lazy
lijep beautiful, handsome
lijepiti to paste
lijevo left
liker liqueur
limun lemon
limunada lemonade
linija line
lipanj June
list sheet, page, leaf

M

list sole (*fish*)
listopad October
litra liter
ljekarna pharmacy
ljepilo glue
ljepljivo sticky
ljepota beauty
ljeto summer
ljevati to pour
ljubav love
ljubazan kind
ljubičast purple
ljubomoran jealous
ljudi men, people
ljut angry
ljutiti se to be angry
lokalni local
lokot padlock
lomiti to rupture
lomljiv breakable, fragile
losos salmon
lopatica shoulder blade
lopov crook, thief
loš bad
loš san nightmare
loša probava indigestion
loše badly
loviti to hunt
loza vine
lozovača grape brandy
lubanja skull
lubenica watermelon
lud crazy, mad, insane
luđak fool
luk onion
luka harbor, port
luksuz luxury
luksuzan luxurious
luksuzna kabina stateroom
lula pipe (*smoking*)
lumbago lumbago
lutati to wander
lutka doll

mačka cat
madrac mattress
  zračni madrac air mattress
Mađar(ica) Hungarian
Mađarska Hungary
mađarski Hungarian
magarac donkey
magla fog
maglovito foggy
magnetofon tape recorder
mahati to wave
majica sweatshirt, t-shirt, top
majka mother
majmun monkey
majoneza mayonnaise
majušan tiny
Makedonac, Makedonka Macedonian
Makedonija Macedonia
maksimum maximum
malen little, small
malina raspberry
malo little, few, a bit
manje less
manšeta cuff
marama scarf
maramica handkerchief
marelica apricot
mariniran marinated
marka stamp
marmelada marmalade
maska mask
maskara mascara
maslac butter
maslina olive
maslinovo ulje olive oil
mast grease, lard, ointment
mastan greasy
med honey
medeni mjesec honeymoon
medenjaci honey cookies
medicina medicine (*the study of*)
mediteranski Mediterranean

meduza jellyfish
medvjed bear
među among
međugradski razgovor long-distance
   telephone call
međunarodni international
međuvremenu, u in the meantime
mehaničar mechanic
mekan soft
melodija tune
menikiranje manicure
mesar butcher
meso meat
metal metal
metar meter
metropol metropolis
metvica mint
mi we
migrena migraine
miješana salata mixed salad
miješano meso na žaru
   selection of grilled meats
miješati karte to shuffle cards
milja mile
mineralna voda mineral water
minuta minute
mir i tišina peace and quiet
miran calm, quiet
miris scent, smell
mirodija spice
misliti to think
miš mouse
mišić muscle
mjehur bladder
mjenjačka kutija gearbox
mjerilo gauge
mjeriti to measure
mjesec month, moon
mjesto place
mjesto rođenja place of birth
mješavina mixture
mlad young
mladi krumpir new potatoes
mladić youth (person)

mladost youth (period of life)
mladoženja bridegroom
mlijeko milk
mljeven ground
mnogo much, many
mnoštvo crowd
množiti to multiply
moda fashion
modrica bruise
moguć possible
mogućnost possibility
moj my, mine
moka mocha
mokar wet
molba request
molim please, excuse me,
   you're welcome
moliti se to pray
molo jetty
momčad team
moćan mighty
moći to be able (to)
moped moped
morati to have to
more sea
   kraj mora by the sea
morem by sea
mornar sailor
morska bolest seasickness
morska obala seafront
morska trava seaweed
morski jež sea urchin
morski okunj lumpfish
morski pas shark
morski rakovi sea crabs
morski zrak sea air
most bridge
motocikl motorcycle
motor engine, motor
motorni čamac motorboat
možda maybe
mramor marble
mrav ant
mreža net

mreža za ribanje fishing net
mrkva carrot
mrlja fleck, spot
mršav skinny
mrtav dead
mrtva sezona off season
mržnja hate
mrziti to hate
mučnina nausea
mudrost wisdom
muha fly
mula mule
munja lightning
musaka moussaka
Musliman, Muslimanka Moslem
muslimanski Moslem
mušica gnat
muški men's
muški zahod men's room
mušule mussels
muzej museum

N

na at, on
na gradele barbecued
na primjer for example
na ražnju spit-roasted
na roštilju grilled
na sat per hour
na tucete by the dozen
na ulju cooked in oil
na žaru grilled
nabaviti (što) to obtain
način way, method
naći to find
nad above
nada hope
nadati se to hope
nadimak nickname
nadjeven stuffed
nagrada prize
najbliži rod next of kin
najbolji best
najgori worst

najlon vrećica plastic bag
najmanje least
najmanji smallest, minimum
najnovije the latest thing
najprije firstly
najveći biggest
najviše the most, mostly
nakit jewelry
nakon after
naljepnica label
namjeran intentional
namjerno deliberately
namještaj furniture
namješten furnished
naočale eyeglasses
naopako upside down
napadaj assault
napasti to attack
napisati to write down
naplata fee
naplatiti to charge
napojnica tip *(to waiter, etc.)*
naporno strenuous
napregnuti to exert
naprijed forward
napuniti to fill (up)
naranča orange
naravni odrezak plain veal cutlet
naravno of course
narječje dialect
naročito especially
narodna glazba folk music
narodna nošnja folk costume
narodni običaji folk customs
narodna pjesma folk song
narodni national
narodni ples folk dance
narodnost nationality
naručiti to order
narudžba order
narukvica bracelet
nas us
nastaviti to continue
nastup performance

nastupiti to perform
naš our
naše ours
našto whereupon
nateknut swollen
natenkirati to fill up (*gasoline*)
naticati to swell
natpis sign
naušnica earring
navijač fan (*sports*)
naviti to wind
Nazdravlje! Bless you!
nazvati to call
nažalost alas
ne no, not
ne dirajte do not touch
ne gazi travu keep off the grass
ne, hvala no, thank you
ne naginji se kroz prozor
   do not lean out of window
ne otvaraj vrata dok se vlak ne
zaustavi do not open the door until
   the train has stopped
ne znam I don't know
nebo heaven, sky
nećak nephew
nećakinja niece
nečitak illegible
nedavno recently
nedjelja Sunday
nedruštven antisocial
negdje somewhere
nego than
neiskren insincere
neispravan faulty
neistinit false
neko vrijeme awhile
nekoliko several, a few
nema na čemu don't mention it,
   you're welcome
nemaran careless
nemiran restless
nemoguć impossible
nemoj(te) don't

neobičan extraordinary, unusual
neograničen unlimited
neograničena kilometraža
   unlimited mileage
neopasan harmless
neophodan crucial
neovisan independent
neoženjen unmarried (*man*)
nepomičan stationary
nepravedan unfair
neprekidan perpetual
neprijazan unfriendly
nepristojan indecent
nepromočiv waterproof
nepušače, za non-smoking
nerado unwillingly
neravan uneven
nesanica insomnia
nesporazum misunderstanding
nesreća accident, misfortune
nesreća bad luck
nesretan unhappy
nestati to disappear
nesvjestan unconscious
nesvršen unfinished
nešto something
netko somebody
neudata unmarried (*woman*)
neudoban uncomfortable
neženja bachelor
neugodan unpleasant
neuljudan rude
neurotičan neurotic
neutralan neutral
nevažeći invalid
nevin innocent
nevjerojatan incredible
nevjesta bride
nevolja distress
nezaboravan unforgettable
nezadovoljan dissatisfied
nezaposlen unemployed
nezdrav unhealthy
nezgoda trouble

nezgodan inconvenient
neznanac stranger
ni...ni... neither...nor...
nigdje nowhere
nije za prodaju not for sale
nijedan none
nikada never
nimalo not in the least
ništa nothing
ništica zero
nitko nobody, no one
nizak short *(person)*
nizak low
Njemačka Germany
njemački German
Njemac, Njemica German
nježan delicate
njihov their
njihovo theirs
noga foot, leg
nogomet soccer
nokat fingernail
noktorezac nail clippers
non-stop non-stop
noć night
noćni klub night club
noćni stol night table
noću by night
normalan normal
Norveška Norway
nos nose
nositi to carry, to wear
nošnja costume
nov new
nova godina new year
novčanica note *(monetary)*
novčarka billfold, wallet
novac money
Novi Zeland New Zealand
novine newspaper
nož knife
nožni prst toe
nudistička plaža nudist beach
nuditi to offer

O

o about
obuća footwear
obala coast, shore
obalna straža coastguard
obavezan obligatory
obavijestiti to notify, to inform
obečanje promise
običaj custom
običan usual, ordinary
obično usually
obitelj family
objasniti to explain
objašnjenje explanation
objektiv lens *(photography)*
oblačno cloudy
oblak cloud
oblik shape, form, figure *(person)*
oboje both
obožavati adore
obraz cheek
obrok meal
obrva eyebrow
obući se to dress
ocat vinegar
očekivati to expect
očevidac eyewitness
očigledan obvious
očuvati to preserve
od of, from, since
od...do... from...to...
od svakale from all over
od toga from it
odani, Vaš yours truly
odbitak deduction
odbiti to deduct
odbojnik bumper
odgoda delay
odgoditi to delay
odgovarajuće suitable
odgovarati to answer
　ovo ne odgovara this isn't right
odgovor answer

odgovoran responsible, liable
odijelo suit
odio department, compartment
odjeća clothing
odjeljenje ward, department
odlazak *(pl. odlasci)* departure
odlučiti to decide
odluka decision
odmah immediately
odmah preko just across
odmarati se to rest
odmor rest, vacation
odnijeti to carry away
odobrenje permission
odobriti to approve
odrastao adult *(adj.)*
određen definite
odrezak cutlet
odsutan absent
odustati to give up
odvezati to untie
odvjetnik attorney
odvodna cijev drain
odvojen separate
odvratan disgusting
oglas advertisement
ograda fence
ograničenje brzine speed limit
ograničeno limited
ogrlica necklace
ogroman enormous
ogrozd gooseberry
ogrtač overcoat
ogrtač za kupanje bathrobe
ohlađen chilled
oklada bet
oko eye
ok(olo) around, about
okrenuti to turn, to start a car
okrugao round
okusiti to taste
okužen polluted
okvir frame
olakšati to lighten *(a load)*

olovka pencil
oluja storm
omladinski hotel youth hostel
omlet omelet
omot wrapping
omotnica envelope
on he
ona she
onaj that one
onda then
onesvijestiti se to faint
oni they, those
ono it
opasan dangerous
opasnost danger
opasnost od požara danger of fire
opaziti to notice
opeklina od sunca sunburn
opekotina burn
opeći se to burn oneself
operacija operation
opet again
opis description
općinski municipal
opkoliti to surround
oprema equipment
oprezan careful
opreznost caution
oprostite excuse me
oprostiti to forgive
opruge točkova suspension *(auto)*
optičar optician
optimistički optimistic
opustiti se to relax
orah walnut
orahnjača walnut roll
orao eagle
orasi walnuts
organizacija organization
organizirati to organize
originalan original
orkestar band *(musical)*
ormar closet, cupboard
osa wasp

osamljen secluded
osigurač fuse
osiguranje insurance
osim except, besides
osim toga furthermore
osip rash
osjećajan sensitive
osjećati to feel
osjećati to sense
oslić hake
oslobođeno carine duty-free
osnivač founder
osnovni basic
osoba person
osobni personal
osovina axle
ospice measles
ostati to remain
ostaviti to leave
ostvariti to realize
osvježavajući refreshing
oštar sharp
oštećeno damaged
oštetiti to damage
otac father
otići to leave, to go away
otkaz cancellation
otkazati to cancel
otključati to unlock
otkopčati to undo
otmjen posh
otok island
otpakovati to unpack
otpasti to come off
otprilike approximately
otputovati to depart
otraga in the back
otrcan scruffy
otresti to shake off
otrovan poisonous
otrovanje želuca food poisoning
otvarač opener
otvoren open
otvoriti to open

ova(j) this
ovamo here
ovca sheep
ovdje here
ovi these
ovisiti to depend
ovo this
ovratnik collar
ozbiljan serious
oznaka mark
oženjen married *(man)*
ožujak March

P

pacijent patient *(medical)*
padati snijeg to snow
padati kiša to rain
paket package, parcel
pakovati to pack
palača palace
palačinka pancake, crêpe
palac thumb
palenta polenta
paljenje ignition
palma palm tree
paluba deck
pametan smart
pamuk cotton
panika panic
panj log
papa pope
papar pepper
papir paper
papirnica stationery store
paprike peppers
par couple, pair
paralelan parallel
parfem perfume
park park
parkiralište parking lot
parobrod steamer
pas dog
pasti to fall
pastrva trout

paški sir hard dry cheese from the island of Pag

pašteta paté

pašticada Dalmatian beef stew

patka duck

patlidžan (plavi) eggplant

patnja suffering

patuljak dwarf

pauk spider

pažljiv careful

pčela bee

pecivo roll, bun

pečen fried

pečurke field mushrooms

pekara bakery

pekmez jam

pelene diapers

penjati se to climb

penkala pen

penzioner pensioner

pećnica oven

pepeonik ashtray

peraja flippers

perika wig

perina down comforter

perje feathers

perla pearl

peron platform *(train)*

peršun parsley

perut dandruff

peta heel

petak Friday

petrolej kerosene

pidžama pajamas

pijaca market

pijesak sand

piknik picnic

pile(tina) chicken

pile na roštilju barbecued chicken

pileća juha chicken soup

pilula pill

pinceta tweezers

piće beverage

pipa faucet

pirjan braised

pisac writer

pisanje writing

pisaći stol desk

pisaći stroj typewriter

pisati to write

pismo letter

pita pie

pita od jabuka Croatian apple pie

pitanje question

pitati to ask

piti to drink

pivo beer

pizza pizza

pjeskovit sandy

pjesma song

pjesnik poet

pješačiti to go on foot, to hike

pješački prijelaz pedestrian crossing

pješak pedestrian

pjevač singer

pjevati to sing

plahta sheet

plakati to cry

plamen flame

plan grada street map

planina mountain

planinar mountain climber

planirati to plan

plastika plastic

platiti to pay

plav blue

plavuša blonde

plaža beach

ples dance

plesač(ica) dancer

plesati to dance

pletenje knitting

plin gas *(natural or butane)*

plitak shallow

plivanje swimming

plivati to swim

pljeskavica Croatian grilled hamburger

ploča record

pločnik sidewalk
plovak buoy
pluća lungs
po narudžbi custom-made
po osobi per person
pobijediti to conquer, to win
poboljšati to improve
pobrinuti se za to attend to
pocrniti to tan
početak beginning, start
početi to begin
pod floor
poderati to rip, to tear
podesiti to adjust
podkošulja undershirt
podmazati to grease
podmiriti (dug) to settle (a debt)
podne noon
područje area, region
podrum cellar
podsjetiti (koga) to remind
podstava lining
podsuknja slip *(clothing)*
poduljiti to lengthen
poduzeće firm *(company)*
poduzeti to undertake
podvarak roast meat on sauerkraut
podzemni underground
pogačica Croatian biscuit
pogačica s čvarcima
  pork crackling biscuit
pogled view
pogodan convenient
pogoditi to guess
pogoršati se to get worse
pogreb funeral
pohan breaded and fried
pohvaliti to praise
pojačan fortified
pokazati prstom to point
pokazati to show
poklade carnival (mardi gras)
poklon gift
poklopac lid

pokraj beside, next to
pokrasti to rob
pokret motion
pokretač starter
pokriti to cover
pokupiti to pick up
pokušaj attempt
pokušati to attempt, to try
pokvaren želudac upset stomach
pola half
polako slowly
polemički controversial
polica shelf
policajac policeman
policija police
polirati to polish
polje field
Poljska Poland
poljubac kiss
poljubiti to kiss
polovan second-hand
polovica half
polubrat half-brother
poluga mjenjača gearshift
polupansion half board
pomfrit french fries
pomoć help
pomoći to help
pomoćnik assistant
ponašanje behavior
ponedjeljak Monday
ponekad sometimes
ponijeti sa sobom to bring along
ponoć midnight
ponosan proud
ponoviti to repeat
ponovo again
popust discount
poriluk leek
poplava flood
popravci repairs
popraviti to repair, to mend
popravljen repaired
popularan popular

popust discount
poraz defeat
porculan china, porcelain
poreći to deny
portir porter
Portugal Portugal
(po)rub hem
poruka note, message
posao job, business deal, work
poseban special
posjedovati to own
posjet visit
posjetiti to visit
posjetnica business card
posladiti to sweeten
poslanik ambassador
poslanstvo embassy
poslastica dessert
poslati to send
poslije after
poslije podne afternoon
poslovica proverb
poslovna zgrada office building
poslovni čovjek businessman
poslovno putovanje business trip
posluga service
poslužiti to serve
pospan sleepy
posrednik middleman
postaja station
postati to become
postelja bed
posteljina bed linen
postojati to exist
postolar shoemaker
postotak per cent
postupati to act
postupno gradually
posuda dish
posuditi to borrow
pošiljka shipment
pošta mail, post office
poštanski pretinac P.O. Box
poštanski sanduk mail box

poštanski broj zip code
poštarina (za) postage rates (for)
pošten honest
poštovanjem, s respectfully
poticati to encourage
potišten depressed
potok stream
potpis signature
potpisati to sign
potpun complete, whole
potreban necessary
potres mozga concussion
potvrda certificate
potvrditi to confirm
poučan instructive
pouzdan dependable, reliable
povećanje enlargement *(of photo)*
povećati to increase, to enlarge
povijest history
povisiti to raise
povisiti cijenu to raise the price
povjesni historical
povjetarac breeze
povraćati to vomit
povratak return
povratiti to return
povratiti to vomit
povremeno occasionally
povrijeda injury
povrijeđen injured
povrće vegetables
povučen shy
pozadi behind
pozdraviti to greet, to send greetings to
pozivni broj area code
pozivnica invitation
poznat familiar, known
poznati to know *(a person)*
pozornica stage
pozvati to call up, to invite
požar! fire!
požarna uzbuna fire alarm
požarne stube fire escape
aparat za gašenje požara

fire extinguisher
praonica laundry, laundromat
prasetina suckling pig
prati to wash
pratiti to accompany
pravedan just *(proper)*
pravi genuine
pravilan correct
pravosuđe justice
prazan empty
prebivalište address
prebrojiti to count it
pred in front of
predak ancestor
predati to hand over
predati prtljagu to check luggage
predavanje lecture
predgrađe suburb
predjelo appetizer
predlagati to suggest
predmet article
prednji front
predosjećaj premonition
predstaviti (se) to introduce (oneself)
predstavnik representative
predvorje lobby
pregled examination *(medical)*
pregledati to examine
pregrijati to overheat
prejako overpowering
prekinuti to interrupt
prekjučer day before yesterday
preko across, over, via
preko noći overnight
preksutra day after tomorrow
prekuhan overcooked
prema toward, according to
prema gore upward
prenijeti to carry over
preći to cross
preosvjetljen overexposed
prepisati to transcribe
preporučeno by registered mail
preporučiti to recommend

preporuka recommendation
prepoznati to recognize
presaviti to fold
preseliti to move
prestati to stop
prestrašen horrified
prestrašiti to shock
pretežak overweight
pretinac locker
preuzeti to take over
prevariti to cheat
prevladati to prevail
prevoditelj(ica) translator
prevoditi to translate
prevrnuti se to capsize
prezime last name, surname
pribadača pin
približiti se to approach
pribor za ribanje fishing tackle
pribor za jelo cutlery
priča story
pričati to chat
prigušivač muffler
prihvatiti to accept
prijatelj(ica) friend
prijateljski friendly
prijateljstvo friendship
prijava registration form
prijaviti to declare *(customs)*
prijaviti se (u hotel)
    to check into a hotel
prije before
prijelaz crossing
prijem reception
prijepodne forenoon
prijesan raw
prijevara fraud
prijevod translation
priključiti se to join
prikolica trailer
prilog side dish
prileći to take a nap
priličan considerable, substantial
prilično quite

prilika situation, opportunity
primaća soba living room
primiti to receive, to accept
primjer example
prići to approach
pripadati to belong
pripaziti to keep an eye on
priprema preparation
pripremiti to prepare
priroda nature
prirodan natural
prisiliti to force
pristanište dock
prisustvovati to attend
pritisak ulja oil pressure
pritisnuti to press
privatan private
privlačan attractive
privremen temporary
prizemlje ground floor
priznanica receipt
priznati to admit
prljav dirty
probava digestion
probiti to penetrate
problem problem
probuditi to wake up
probušen punctured
probušiti to puncture
proći to pass, to go by
prodaja sale
prodavati to sell
program program
proizvod product
prokule brussels sprouts
prolaz passage, alley
proljeće spring *(season)*
proljev diarrhea
promašiti to miss
promet traffic
prometan crowded, busy (place)
promijeniti to change
promjena change
propusnica permit

prosinac December
prositi to beg
prosječan average
proslava celebration
proslijediti to proceed
prospekt leaflet
prostitutka prostitute
prostor space
prosuti to spill
prošetati se to take a walk, to stroll
prošlost past
protestant Protestant
protiv against
provalnik burglar
provjeriti to check
prozor window
prsluk vest
prst finger
prstaci mussels
prsten ring
pršut Dalmatian ham
prtljaga luggage
prtljažnik trunk *(auto)*
prugast striped
prva pomoć first aid
    pribor za prvu pomoć first aid kit
prvenstvo priority
prvi first
prvi razred first class
pržen fried
pržiti to fry
psovka swearword
ptica bird
pučanstvo population
publika audience
puder powder
puding pudding
puknut cracked
pumpa pump
pumpati to pump
pun full
punac father-in-law
puni pansion full board
puno much, full

puretina turkey *(meat)*
pustiti vodu flush *(a toilet)*
pušiti to smoke
put route, path, way
putna karta road map
putnička agencija travel agency
putnička torba traveling bag
putnički ček traveler's check
putnik passenger
putovanje journey, trip, tour
putovati to travel
putovnica passport
puzati to crawl

R

rabin rabbi
račići prawns
račun receipt, bill
računalo computer
računar calculator
radije rather *(instead)*
radilica crankshaft
raditi to work
radni dani working days
radno vrijeme office hours, working hours
radost joy
radostan glad
radoznao inquisitive
rajčica tomato
rak crab
rakija brandy
rame shoulder
rano early
rasa race *(people)*
raskrsnica crossroads, intersection
raspasti se to fall apart
raspoloženje mood
raspored schedule, itinerary, timetable
rasprodaja clearance sale
rasprodano sold out
rastegnuti to stretch
rastopiti to dissolve

rastrgati to tear apart
rastrošan wasteful
rat war
ratluk Turkish delight
ravan straight, direct, flat
ravno naprijed straight ahead
ravnopravnost equality
razdoblje period *(of time)*
razgledavanje sightseeing
razglednica post card
razjasniti to clarify
različit different
razlika difference
razmijeniti to give change
razno assorted
razočaran disappointed
razonoda amusement
razred class
razuman sensible, understanding
razumijeti to understand
razveden divorced
razveseliti to make happy
razviti (film) to develop (film)
razvodnik distributor *(auto)*
raženi kruh rye bread
ražnjići kebobs
rebra ribs
recepcija reception desk *(hotel)*
recept prescription, recipe
reći to say, to tell
red line, queue, row
red letenja flight schedule
red vožnje timetable
redarstvena ispostava police station
redarstvenik policeman
redarstvo police
regenerator hair conditioner
reket racket
reklama advertisement
reklamacije complaints
remek-djelo masterpiece
remen belt
remen ventilatora fan belt
rendgenske zrake X-ray

renesansa Renaissance
restoran restaurant
retrovizor rearview mirror
reuma rheumatism
rezanci noodles
rezati to cut
rezbar engraver
rezervacija reservation
rezervirati to reserve
rezervna guma spare tire
rezervni djelovi spare parts
rezultat result, score *(sports)*
riba fish
  loviti ribu to fish
ribanje fishing
ribar fisherman
ribarnica fish market
ribarski čamac fishing boat
ribizli red currants
riblji restoran seafood restaurant
ribolov fishing
ričet thick barley soup
riječ word
rijedak rare, thin
rijeka river
rijetko seldom
Rim Rome
riskantan risky
riskirati to risk
riva promenade
rizi-bizi rice and peas
riža rice
rižoto risotto (rice in rich meat or seafood sauce)
rječnik dictionary
rješiti se to resolve, to get rid of
roba goods
robna kuća department store
rodbina relatives
roditelji parents
rođak relative, cousin *(male)*
rođakinja cousin *(female)*
rođen born
rođendan birthday

rok term
rok trajanja... sell by...
rolat roll (cake)
romanski Romanesque
ronjenje scuba diving
roštilj barbecue, grill
rotkvica radish
rub brim
rubeola German measles
ručak lunch
ručica lever
ručka handle
ručna kočnica handbrake
ručna prtljaga hand luggage
ručni rad handmade
ručni sat wrist watch
ručni zglob wrist
ručnik towel
rujan September
ruka arm, hand
rukav sleeve
rukavice gloves
rukopis handwriting
rukotvorine crafts
rukovati se to shake hands
rukovodstvo management
ruksak backpack
rum rum
rumenilo blusher
rupa hole
Rus Russian
Rusija Russia
ruski Russian
ruševine ruins
ruž za usne lipstick
ruža rose
ružan ugly
ružica rosette, rosé wine
ružičasta boja pink

S

s(a) with
sada now
  za sada for now

sadašnjost the present
sadašnja vremena modern times
sagnuti se to bend over
(sa)graditi to build
saharin saccharine
sajam fair (commercial)
sako blazer
sakriti to hide
sakupiti to gather
sakupljati to collect
sala hall
salata salad
salo flab
sam alone
samilost compassion
samo just, only
samoposluga self-service, supermarket
samostan monastery
samt velvet
san dream
sandale sandals
sanjati to dream
sapun soap
sardelice anchovies
sardine sardines
sarma stuffed cabbage rolls
sastanak meeting
sastav composition
sasvim completely
sat clock, hour
sataraš onion, tomato and sweet
   pepper omelet
sauna sauna
sav entire, all
savijača strudel
savitljiv flexible
savjetovati to advise
savršen perfect
sedlo saddle
sef safe *(n.)*
sekelji gulaš pork and sauerkraut
   goulash
seks sex
sekunda second *(time)*

seljak farmer
selo village
semafor traffic light
sendvič sandwich
senf mustard
senzacionalan sensational
sestra sister
sestrična cousin *(female)*
sezona season
SIDA AIDS
sidrište moorings
sidro anchor
siguran certain, safe
sigurno certainly, definitely
sigurnosni pojas seatbelt
siječanj January
silan terrific, tremendous
silovanje rape
silovati to rape
simpatičan nice
sin son
sinagoga synagogue
sintetičan synthetic
sići to get down
sipa cuttlefish
sir cheese
sirnica cheese pie
siromašan poor
sitniš small change
siv gray
sjaj za usne lip gloss
sjajan bright
sjećati se to remember
Sjedinjene Američke Države (SAD)
   United States of America
sjedište seat
sjediti to sit
sjenilo za oči eye shadow
sjenovit shady
sjesti to sit down
sjever north
skakati to jump
skije skis
skijanje skiing

skijanje na vodi water skiing
skijaška žičara ski lift
skijaške cipele ski boots
skijati se to ski
skinuti to take off
skladatelj composer
skladati to compose
sklonište shelter
skoro almost, nearly
skrenuti to turn
skretanje turning
skup expensive
skupiti se to shrink
skuša mackerel
slab weak, flimsy
sladak sweet
sladoled ice cream
   kornet sladoleda ice cream cone
slanina bacon
slano salty
slapovi falls
slastičarna pastry shop
slatkiši sweets
slatko sweet fruit preserve
slava glory
sličan similar
slijedeći next
slijediti to follow
slijep blind
slijepa točka blind spot
slika picture, painting
slikar painter
slikati to paint
slobodan free, available, vacant
slomiti to break, to fracture
slomljen broken
Slovenac, Slovenka Slovene
Slovenija Slovenia
slovenski slovenian
slon elephant
slučaj case, chance
   u slučaju in case
   u svakom slučaju in any case
slučajnost coincidence

slušati to listen
službeni official
smanjite brzinu reduce speed
smeće rubbish, litter
smeđ brown
smetati to bother, to disturb
smetnja nuisance
smijati se to laugh
smijeh laughter
smiješak smile
smiješan funny
smiješiti se to smile
smještaj accomodations
smjer direction
smoking dinner jacket
smokva fig
smračiti se to get dark
smrditi to stink
smrt death
smrznut frozen
smuđ perch
snaga power, strength
snaha daughter-in-law
snažan strong, powerful
snijeg snow
sniziti cijenu to discount
sniženje reduction
soba room
soba za gosta guest room
sobarica chambermaid
sobe za izdavanje rooms to let
sok juice
sol salt
solidan solid
som catfish
sparno humid, muggy
spasiti to save, to rescue
spavanje sleep
spavaća kola sleeper car
spavaća soba bedroom
spavati to sleep
specijalitet delicacy, specialty
spisak list
splav catamaran

spojiti to connect
spol sex *(gender)*
spomenik monument
spomenuti to mention
spor slow
spreman prepared
sprski Serbian
spustiti slušalicu to hang up *(telephone)*
spužva sponge
srčani napad heart attack
sramota shame
Srbija Serbia
srce heart
srdačan cordial
srdačno heartily
srebro silver
sredina center, middle
srednje pečeno medium-rare
srednji central
srednji vijek Middle Ages
srednjovjekovni medieval
sredstvo means
sreća happiness, luck
srećom fortunately
sretan happy, lucky, fortunate
Sretan Božić Merry Christmas
srijeda Wednesday
srljati to rush
srnetina venison
srpanj July
srušiti se to collapse
stajati to cost
stajati to stand
stajalište taksija taxi stand
staklo glass
stalan permanent
stambena zgrada apartment house
stan apartment
stanar tenant
stanje condition
   u drugom stanju pregnant
stanovati to reside
stanovnik inhabitant
star old, stale

staromodan old-fashioned
stati to stop
staviti na kreditnu karticu to charge
   on a credit card
staviti to place, to put
staza path
stećak old Bosnian tombstone
stil style
stisnuti to tighten
stol table
stolar carpenter
stolica chair
stoljeće century
stolni tenis table tennis
stolnjak tablecloth
stolno vino table wine
stomatolog dentist
stopirati to hitchhike
strah fear
stran foreign
strana side
strana valuta foreign currency
stranac foreigner
strani jezik foreign language
strašan awful, terrible
stražnja vrata back door
stražnje sjedište back seat
stražnji back (rear)
stric uncle (father's brother)
strina aunt
strm steep
stroj za pranje rublja washing
   machine
strop ceiling
strpljiv patient
stručnjak expert
stručno technical
struja electricity
struk waist
stube stairs
stubište staircase
studeni November
stupanj degree *(temperature)*
stupiti u vezu to contact

stvar thing
stvaran real
stvarno really
stvarnost reality
subota Saturday
sud court of law
sudar crash, collision
sudbina fate
sudionik partner
sudjelovati to participate
sudoper sink
suha šljiva prune
suknja skirt
sukob conflict
suma amount
sumnjiv suspicious
sunce sun
suncobran beach umbrella
suncokret sunflower
sunčane naočale sunglasses
sunčano sunny
sunčati se to sunbathe
suosjećajnost sympathy
super super, premium gas
suprotan opposite
suprug husband, spouse
supruga wife, spouse
suputnik fellow traveler
susjed neighbor
susjedna next door
susjedstvo neighborhood
sutra tomorrow
suvenir souvenir
suvremen contemporary, modern
suvremena umjetnost modern art
suza tear
suženje ceste road narrows
svakako by all means
svaki every, each
svatko everyone
sve everything
svećenik priest
svega i svačega all kinds of things
svekar father-in-law

svekrva mother-in-law
sveopći general
svet holy
svetište shrine
sveučilište university
sveukupno altogether, total
svi all, everybody
svibanj May
svijeća candle
svijet world
svijetliti to light
svijetlo light
svijetski rat world war
svila silk
svinjetina pork
svinjska krmenadla pork chop
svirati to play an instrument
svječica spark plug
svjedok witness
svjetionik lighthouse
svjetlomjer exposure meter
svjež fresh, breezy
svježe *(weather)* cool
svježe obojano wet paint
svota amount, sum
svrbiti to itch
svuda everywhere
svući to take off

šah chess
šal shawl
šala joke
šalica cup
šaliti se to joke
šampanjac champagne
šampon shampoo
šaptati to whisper
šaran carp
šarmantan charming *(person)*
šasija chassis
šator tent
šatobrijan chateaubriand
šaumpita flaky pastry with meringue

šav seam
šećer sugar
šef boss
šešir hat
šeri sherry
šetanje a walk, a stroll
šetati se to go for a walk
šišanje haircut
širok broad, wide
šivati to sew
škampi scampi
škare scissors
školjka shell
škola school
Škotska Scotland
šlag whipped cream
šlepati to tow
šlic fly *(on trousers)*
šljiva plum
šljivovica plum brandy
šminka make-up
šmirgla emery board
šnenokle snow eggs *(dessert)*
šoferska ploča dashboard
šogorica sister-in-law
šok shock
šokantan shocking
špaga string
špagete spaghetti
Španjolac Spaniard
Španjolska Spain
španjolski spanish
šparoga asparagus
špilja cave
špinat spinach
šport sport
štaka crutch
štakor rat
štanglice bar cookies
štap za ribanje fishing rod
štediti to save
štednjak stove
šteta damage, harm
šteta! what a shame!

štetan harmful
štipati to pinch
štititi to protect
štrudla strudel
štruklji salty cheese-filled strudel
štucanje hiccups
štuka pike
šuma forest, woods
šunka ham
šurjak brother-in-law
Švedska Sweden
švedski Swedish
Šveđanin, Šveđanka Swede
Švicarska Switzerland
švicarski Swiss

T

tablete tablets, pills
tacna tray
taj that one
tajiti to keep secret
tajna secret
takav such
tako so
također also, too
taksi taxi
taksi stajalište taxi stand
taksimetar taximeter
taksista taxi driver
Talijan Italian
talijanski Italian
talk talcum powder
taman dark
tamo there
tamponi tampons
tanak thin
tanjur plate
tanjurić saucer
tarana grated dough
tava frying pan
tečaj course
tečno fluently
tek appetite
tek just

tekući puder foundation (*make-up*)
teleći (*adj.*) veal
telefon telephone, brzoglas
telefonirati to telephone
telefonski imenik telephone book
telegram telegram
teleobjektiv telephoto lens
teletina veal
televizor television
temperatura temperature
tempo pace
tenis tennis
tenis igralište tennis court
tenisice sneakers
tentati to tease
tepih carpet, rug
terasa terrace, patio
teret freight
teretni brod freighter
teretni vlak freight train
termometar thermometer
termos thermos
termostat thermostat
teškoća difficulty
teta aunt
tetak uncle (*aunt's husband*)
težak heavy, difficult
težina weight
težiti za to strive for
ti you (*singular & familiar*)
tifus typhoid
tigar tiger
tih quiet
tijelo body
tinta ink
tišina silence
tipičan typical
tiskanice forms, prined matter
tiskati to print
titlovan with subtitles
tjedan week
tjesan tight
tkanina fabric
tko who

tko bilo whoever
tlačiti to oppress
to je toliko that is that much
to that
toaletni papir toilet paper
tobože supposedly
točan accurate, exact, correct, punctual
točka dot
tona ton
tonik tonic
topao warm
toplice spa, thermal springs
toranj tower
torba purse, handbag, bag
torta cake, torte
tovar freight
trag trace
trajekt ferry
trajna permanent wave
tramvaj streetcar
transformator transformer
tranzmisija transmission (*auto*)
traper denim
traperice jeans
trapist sir trappiste cheese (*like Port du Salut*)
trava grass
travanj April
tražiti to look for, to search, to ask for
trčati to run
trebati to need
trenirka track suit
trenutak moment
treći third
treći razred third class
trećina a third
trešnja cherry
trg square (*city*)
trgovac dealer
trgovina shop, store
tri three
trijezan sober
trka race

tronožac tripod
tropski tropical
trošiti to spend
truba horn *(auto)*
trvenje friction
tržnica market
tucet dozen
tuča fight
tučeno vrhnje whipped cream
tulipan tulip
tumač interpreter
tumačiti to interpret
tunel tunnel
tunina tuna fish
Turčin Turk
turist tourist
turizam tourist trade
turpija za nokte nail file
Turska Turkey
turska kava Turkish coffee
turski Turkish
tuš shower
tužan sad
tužiti to sue
tvar matter
tvoj your
tvoje yours
tvornica factory
tvrd firm, hard
tvrđava fortress

u

u slast! bon appétit!
u at, in. into
u kvaru out of order
u prolazu in passing
u redu okay
u zadnje vrijeme lately
ubiti to kill
ubosti to prick, to sting
ubrus napkin
ući to enter, to go in, to get in
učenik pupil
učitelj(ica) teacher

učiti to learn, to study
udaljen remote
udariti to hit, to strike, to bump
udata married *(woman)*
udica fish-hook
udoban comfortable, cozy
udovac widower
udovica widow
uđite bez kucanja
    enter without knocking
uganuti to sprain, to twist
ugao corner
ugasiti to switch off
ugled reputation
ugodan pleasant
ugovor contract
ugovoreno it's a deal
ugovoriti sastanak make a date
ugristi to bite
ugriz bite
uhapsiti to arrest
uho ear
uhvatiti to catch
ujak uncle *(mother's brother)*
ujediniti to unite
ujna aunt
ujutro a.m., in the morning
uključiti to include
ukočen numb, stiff
ukoliko if, inasmuch
ukraden stolen
ukras decoration, ornament
ukrasti to steal
ukus flavor, taste
ukusan delicious
ulaz admission, entrance
ulaz na druga vrata use other door
ulaznica admission ticket
ulica street
ulje oil
uljudan polite
uložiti to deposit
umak sauce
umak od mesa gravy

umirovati se to retire
umirovljen retired
umjeren reasonable
umjesto instead
umjetan artificial
umjetnički artistic
umjetničko djelo work of art
umjetnik artist
umjetnost art
umoran tired
umotati to wrap
umrijeti to die
unaprijed in advance
uništiti to destroy
unuk grandson
unuka granddaughter
unutra inside
upala inflammation
upala pluća pneumonia
upala grla strep throat
upalite svijetla switch on your headlights
upaliti to inflame
upaliti to switch on
upaljač lighter
uporaba use
upoznati to meet, to make one's acquaintance
upozorenje warning
uprava management
upravitelj manager
upravljač steering wheel
uputiti na to refer to
urar watchmaker
ured office
uredan neat
urmašice Bosnian cookies in syrup
uručiti to hand to
usamljen lonely
usisavač vacuum cleaner
uskoro soon
Uskrs Easter
usna lip
uspješan successful

usporedba comparison
usprkos in spite of
usta mouth
usuditi se to dare
utičnica outlet *(electrical)*
utikač plug *(electric)*
utisak impression
utjecaj influence
utorak Tuesday
utrnuti to go numb
uvijek always
uvoz import
uvoziti to import
uvrijeda offense, insult
uvrijediti to offend, to insult
uz along
uzak narrow
uzalud in vain
uzbuđen excited
uzbuna alarm
uzburkan rough *(sea)*
uzeti to take
uzice laces *(shoe)*
uzimati poslije jela to be taken after meals
uzimati prema priloženom uputstvu to be taken according to enclosed instructions
uzimati prije jela to be taken before meals
uzimati ... puta na dan to be taken ... times per day
uzimati svakih ... sati to be taken every ... hours
uzletište airport
uzrok cause
užasan appalling, horrible
užitak pleasure
uživati to enjoy

V

vadičep corkscrew
vagon restoran restaurant car
val wave

valcer waltz
valjušci dumplings
valuta currency
van out
vani outside
vanilice crescent vanilla cookies
vanilija vanilla
vanjska kabina outside cabin
vanjska trgovina foreign trade
vansezonske cijene low season rates
Vaš your
Vaše yours
vatra fire
vatrogasna postaja fire station
vaza vase
važan important
važeći valid
važi do ... expiration date ...
važnost importance
večer evening
večera dinner, supper
večeras tonight
već already, yet
veći bigger
vedro bucket
vegeterijanac vegetarian
veličina size
velik big, large, great, grand
velika slova capital letters
Velika Britanija Great Britain
velikodušan generous
veljača February
ventilator fan, ventilator
veoma very
veselje joy
veseo cheerful, merry
veslo paddle, oar
vesta cardigan
veterinar veterinarian
vez embroidery
veza contact, connection
vezica za cipele shoelace
vežite pojase fasten your seatbelts
Vi you (formal & polite)

vidjeti to see
vijećanje conference
vijećnica, gradska town hall
vijesti news
vijugav winding
vikati to cry, to shout
vikend weekend
vila villa
vilica fork, jaw
vinjak wine brandy
vino wine
vinograd vineyard
vinska karta wine list
visina height
visiti to hang
viski whiskey
visok high, tall
više more
višnje sour cherries
vitak slim
vitamini vitamins
vitez knight
vitleri hair curlers
viza visa
vjenčanje wedding
vjenčati se to get married
vjera religion
vjerojatno probably
vjerovati to believe
vješalica hanger
vještak connoisseur
vjetar wind
vjetrovit windy
vježbati to practice
vlada government
vlak train
vlasnik owner
vlasti authorities
vlažan damp
voće fruit
voćna salata fruit salad
voda water
vodič guide, guidebook
voditi to lead

vodoinstalater plumber
vodoskok fountain
vojni military
vojnik soldier
vojska army
volja will
voljeti to love, to like, to be fond of
voltaža voltage
votka vodka
vozač driver
vozač kamiona truck driver
vozačka iskaznica driver's license
voziti to drive
voziti se to ride
voziti okolo to ride around
vrag devil
vrat neck
vrata door
vratiti (se) to return
vratiti novac to refund
vrhnje sweet cream
vrijednost value, worth
vrijeme time, weather
vrisnuti to scream
vrlo very
vrpca ribbon, tape
vrsta kind, type
vrt garden
vrtoglavica dizziness
vruč hot
vručina heat
vuci! pull!
vući to pull
vuna wool

Z

za vrijeme during
za for
zabava party, entertainment
zabaviti se to amuse oneself
zabavni park amusement park
zabavno fun, entertaining
zaboravan forgetful

zaboraviti to forget
zabraniti to forbid
zabranjen pristup no admittance
zabranjen prolaz keep out
zabranjen ulaz no entry
zabranjeno... no ...
zabuna mix up
začin salad dressing, seasoning
začiniti to spice
začuđujući amazing
zadnji last, final
zadovoljan content, satisfied
zadovoljavajuće satisfactory
zadovoljiti to satisfy
zaglavljen stuck
zahod toilet, restroom
zahvalan grateful, thankful
zahvaliti se to thank
zajednički mutual, in common
zajedno together
zakletva vow
zakon law
zakopčati to fasten, to buckle up
zakuska appetizer
zalazak sunca sunset
zaljev bay
zalogaj snack
zamamno tempting
zamijeniti to exchange
zamrznut frozen
zanimanje occupation
zanimljiv interesting
zaobilazni put detour
zapad west
zapadni western
zapanjujući astonishing
zapravo in fact
zaraza infection
zarazan infectious
zaručen engaged *(to be married)*
zaručnica fiancée
zaručnik fiancé
zasada for the time being
zaspati to fall asleep

zaštitni znak trade mark
zašto why
zato therefore
zatvaraj vrata please close the door
zatvor prison
zatvoren closed
zatvoreni bazen outdoor swimming pool
zatvoriti to close
zaušnjaci mumps
zauzet busy
zauzeti to occupy
zavezati to shut up
zaveži! shut up!
zavjese drapes, curtains
zavjetovati se to vow
zavoj bandage, dressing on wound
zavoj turn (in road)
završiti to end
zbog since, because of
zbog toga for that reason
zbogom goobye
zbrojiti to add up
zbuniti to confuse
zdenac well
zdrav healthy
zdravica toast (drink)
zdravlje health
zečevina rabbit meat
zelen green
zelena salata lettuce
zelje cabbage
zemička roll, bun
zemlja earth, land
zemljovid map
zet son-in-law
zglob joint (anat.)
zgodan good looking, cute
zid wall
ziherica safety pin
zima winter
zimovanje winter holiday
zlato gold (adj.)

zlo evil
zmija snake
značajan significant
značiti to mean
znak signal
znamenitost interest (place of)
znamenitosti sights
znanje knowledge
znanost science
znati to know (a fact)
znojiti se to perspire
zobeno brašno oatmeal
zoološki vrt zoo
zora dawn
zračna luka airfield
zračni madrac air mattress
zračna pošta airmail
zračnom poštom by airmail
zrak air
zrakoplov airplane
zrcalo mirror
zreo ripe
zub tooth
zubalo denture
zubar dentist
zubni desni gums (dental)
zubobolja toothache
zum-objektiv zoom lens
zvati to call
zvijer animal
zvijezda star
zvoniti to ring
zvono bell

Ž

žaba frog
žalba complaint
žaliti se to complain
žalost, na unfortunately
žao mi je I am sorry
žarulja light bulb
želja desire, wish
željeti to wish
željeznički kolodvor railroad station

željeznički prijelaz railroad crossing
željeznica railroad
želudac stomach
žena woman, wife
ženski ladies', ladies' room
žestoka pića spirits *(drinks)*
žica wire
Židov Jew
židovski Jewish
žigica match
žilav tough
žilet razor blade
živ alive
živac nerve
živčan nervous
živjeli! cheers!

živjeti to live
živo live, lively
život life
žlica spoon
žličica teaspoon
žlijezda gland
žnirati to lace
žnjirač shoelace
žohar cockroach
žrtva victim
žučni kamenac gallstone
žulj blister
žuriti to hurry
žut yellow
žutica jaundice
žvakaća guma chewing gum

Please	**Molim Vas.**
Thank you.	**Hvala.**
Yes. No.	**Da. Ne.**
Excuse me.	**Oprostite.**
Waiter!	**Konobare!**
How much is that?	**Koliko je to?**
Where are the toilets?	**Gdje su zahodi?**

ZAHODI
TOILETS

ŽENSKI or Ž

MUŠKI or M

Please help me.	**Molim Vas pomozite mi.**
Can you tell me...?	**Možete li mi reći...**
where/when/ why	**gdje/kada/zašto**
Where is a restaurant?	**Gdje ima restoran?**
Please write it down.	**Molim Vas napišite.**
I don't understand.	**Ja ne razumijem.**
I don't speak Croatian.	**Ja ne govorim hrvatski.**
Do you speak English?	**Govorite li engleski?**